SAM JAFFERSON

Redefine Your Brain Daily

Contents

1

Introduction

Have you ever woken up feeling a weight on your chest, longing for the joy and peace that seem just out of reach? Imagine waking each day ready to embrace life with energy and purpose. Welcome to a journey crafted especially for those who stand at the exciting yet daunting brink of adulthood. This book is not merely a collection of advice but a guide born from understanding the unique pressures faced by young adults today. It speaks directly to college students juggling their academic pursuits with social lives, to fresh graduates entering the workforce, and young professionals navigating their early careers while seeking balance and fulfillment.

As you turn these pages, prepare yourself for a transformative experience that will bring clarity and calm into your everyday life. Our modern world brims with challenges—from maintaining grades in college to answering the many demands of a budding career. Amidst this whirlwind, it can feel nearly impossible to claim even a moment for ourselves—time to breathe, reflect, and truly live with intent and joy. Yet, within the churn of our daily routine lies the key to a more satisfying life: daily habits. How we manage our mornings, our interactions, our thoughts, and our bodies—every small decision contributes to the overarching quality of our lives.

What if I told you that with each new dawn, you have the opportunity to build upon habits that will enhance your mental health and emotional resilience? Picture this: every deliberate action you take, whether it's pausing to savor a cup of tea or choosing a brisk walk over scrolling through social feeds, serves as a cornerstone in developing a mindset geared towards optimism and well-being. Small steps, subtle shifts—these are the building blocks for an existence that feels not only bearable but genuinely vibrant and connected.

In this book, we'll explore the profound impact of nurturing daily habits. These aren't monumental changes requiring exhaustive effort; rather, they are manageable adjustments that breathe positivity into your routine. By embracing practices like mindfulness, gratitude, and effective communication, you become the architect of your own emotional stability. As we delve deeper, you'll discover how each choice can enhance your mood, decrease stress, and ultimately lead to fulfilling connections with those around you.

The path to transformation begins here. Consider this book your toolkit filled with strategies designed to empower you on your quest for happiness, health, and meaningful relationships. Each chapter offers insights and exercises aimed at solidifying your ability to thrive amidst life's countless pressures. From mastering mindfulness techniques to refining emotional intelligence, we're drawing a map for you—a roadmap where every step encourages growth and renewal.

Within these pages, you'll uncover ways to articulate your

needs more effectively, to form relationships that enrich and inspire, and to cultivate a mental landscape where negativity struggles to take root. The journey doesn't promise a life devoid of struggle but equips you with the resilience needed to tackle adversity head-on. Imagine possessing the skills to navigate workplace challenges with composure, or to balance academic demands without sacrificing mental peace. This vision of empowerment is entirely achievable, and it starts with the simple yet powerful shift in recognizing the role of daily habits.

However, knowing what to do is just the beginning. The real magic lies in taking these principles and weaving them seamlessly into your daily life. That's why throughout this book, we'll focus on actionable insights—practical techniques you can start applying today. These aren't abstract theories or complex protocols; they're straightforward actions you can integrate into your life with ease, crafting a stable foundation for enhanced well-being.

In creating this book, we've drawn inspiration from numerous sources, melding scientific research with timeless wisdom to address the distinct milieu of modern adulthood. Whether you're tackling exams, embarking on new professional ventures, or striving to find personal harmony, the tools presented here aim to fortify your journey. Your experiences, fears, and desires shape the narrative, making this more than just another self-help book but a personalized companion for years to come.

Each leap of understanding brings you closer to realizing the profound interconnectedness of mind, body, and environment. As you progress through the chapters, you'll gain perspective on how to harness this interconnectedness, channeling it toward positive change. With dedication, you'll cultivate a lifestyle that resonates with authenticity and joy—a life where stress doesn't overshadow potential and where burdens morph into stepping stones.

The following chapters are layered meticulously to support you through various dimensions of development. We begin with the bedrock of mindfulness, helping you stay present and focused despite distractions. Then, we dig deeper into emotional management, discovering tactics to steer emotions positively. As the book unfolds, you'll learn how to nurture relationships that contribute meaningfully to your happiness, recognize and respond to physical cues of stress, and construct networks of support. Ultimately, every page turned represents a step closer to the holistic growth of mind, heart, and spirit.

Let's embark together on this dynamic journey of self-discovery and improvement. Herein lies the promise of a brighter tomorrow: a future where your actions today create ripples of joy and fulfillment for days to come. With each chapter, allow yourself to transform holistically, honoring your personal evolution and ushering in an era defined not by what weighs you down but by what lifts you up.

2

Understanding Your Mental Landscape

Familiarize Yourself with the Foundational Concepts of Mental Health and Emotional Intelligence

Understanding the foundational concepts of mental health and emotional intelligence is essential for young adults as they navigate the complexities of daily life. In this chapter, we look into how familiarizing ourselves with these concepts can significantly impact our emotional well-being and interpersonal relationships. By delving into the terminology related to mental health, young adults can gain a better grasp of their own experiences and emotions, which aids in building self-awareness and fostering effective communication. This exploration allows us to articulate our feelings more clearly and develop strategies for managing the ups and downs of life. Moreover, it offers insight into recognizing signs that might indicate when professional support is needed, promoting a proactive approach to maintaining mental health.

As you journey through this chapter, you'll encounter discussions on key mental health terms relevant to young adults, such as anxiety, depression, and stress. These insights will help destigmatize mental health issues by empowering individuals with knowledge that aids understanding and expression of personal challenges without fear of judgment. The chapter also highlights the importance of emotional intelligence (EI) in enhancing communication skills and interpersonal relationships. You'll discover how emotional awareness not only enriches your social interactions but also bolsters coping mechanisms needed for stressful situations. By exploring practical techniques, this chapter equips young adults with tools for boosting EI and navigating the transition into adulthood with greater confidence. Through resources like journaling, mindfulness practices, and workshops, you'll find ways to enhance your emotional landscape proactively while fostering resilience and promoting overall well-being.

Define Key Mental Health Terms Relevant to Young Adults

Understanding foundational concepts of mental health and emotional intelligence plays a vital role in our daily lives. As young adults, stepping into the realm of mental well-being requires us to be acquainted with terminology that can aid our path to self-awareness. Being familiar with these terms isn't just about knowing their definitions but truly recognizing how they manifest in our everyday experiences. Learning this language allows us to better understand ourselves and communicate our feelings more articulately.

Mental health encompasses diverse aspects of our lives, impacting how we think, feel, and behave on a daily basis. It's not just about illness or disorder; it includes our emotional resilience, psychological balance, and social wellbeing. This broad scope underscores why it's so significant in our day-to-day interactions and decision-making processes. For instance, understanding what constitutes good mental health helps us manage stress, work productively, and contribute meaningfully to our community. Knowing when we're mentally healthy versus when we might need support is crucial. Recognizing these variations in mental health is key to identifying when professional help might be needed.

The ability to observe fluctuations in our mental health also involves recognizing personal triggers and coping mechanisms. Each person's mental health journey is unique; what affects one person may not affect another. Acknowledging this variability helps us identify patterns that may signify distress, such as persistent sadness or mood swings, which can be early indicators for seeking help. Such knowledge empowers us to reach out sooner rather than later, promoting timely intervention which can make all the difference in one's healing process.

Emotional intelligence (EI) significantly enhances our interpersonal relationships by bolstering communication skills. Essentially, EI involves being aware of, controlling, and expressing one's emotions judiciously and empathetically. This awareness improves our ability to understand others and engage with them on a deeper level. Imagine having a disagreement with a friend or coworker; high EI equips us to navigate such circumstances calmly and effectively by recognizing our emotional responses and modifying our approach accordingly.

Cultivating emotional intelligence requires developing an understanding of our emotions and learning to interpret the non-verbal cues of others. This results in improved conflict resolution and relationship management skills, enhancing both personal and professional interactions. For young adults transitioning into new roles and responsibilities, higher EI can significantly improve leadership abilities and team dynamics, fostering a collaborative environment.

Familiarity with common mental health terms, like anxiety, depression, and stress, is immensely beneficial in articulating personal experiences. Take anxiety, for example—it's more than just feeling nervous before a big test or presentation. Everyone feels anxious from time to time, but for some, these feelings are persistent and overwhelming, potentially leading to avoidance behaviors. Understanding this term's scope helps individuals articulate their experiences, seek appropriate support, and avoid misinterpretations.

Knowing such terms aids in destigmatizing mental health issues, making it easier for those affected to express their challenges without fear of judgment or misunderstanding. When we can accurately describe our thoughts and feelings, we open doors for effective communication with friends, family, healthcare providers, and counselors who can offer support and solutions tailored to our specific needs.

Not only does understanding these terms benefit us personally, but it also allows us to be supportive allies to those around us. We become better listeners, more empathetic peers, and supportive friends, helping to create a culture where discussing mental health is normalized and encouraged.

In the digital age, resources abound to aid young adults in understanding mental health and emotional intelligence. Whether through podcasts, online courses, or books, there is a wealth of information designed to enlighten, encourage, and equip us with the necessary tools. However, it's important to approach such resources with an informed mindset, ensuring that they're evidence-based and credible.

For college students and young professionals, practical approaches can include journaling about daily experiences to track moods and triggers, engaging in mindfulness practices to stay present, and participating in workshops aimed at boosting emotional intelligence. These methods provide structured avenues to explore one's mental health landscape proactively.

Explore the Impact of Emotions on Daily Life

Emotions are powerful forces that significantly influence our behaviors and interactions, both in personal settings and professional environments. For many young adults entering new phases of life—be it college or the workforce—a thorough understanding of how emotions impact their day-to-day activities is crucial for success.

To begin with, let's consider how emotional states affect performance at work or school. Imagine a student facing a complex set of assignments or a professional preparing for an important presentation. In both cases, emotions play a critical role. Positive emotions such as enthusiasm and excitement can enhance creativity, leading to innovative solutions and increased productivity. Conversely, negative emotions like anxiety or frustration might impede one's ability to focus, causing distractions and reducing performance quality.

This brings us to the idea that moods substantially impact focus, productivity, and motivation. A mood can be thought of as a prolonged emotional state that influences how we perceive and react to situations. For instance, starting the day in a cheerful mood can make daily tasks more enjoyable and less burdensome. However, if someone begins their day feeling stressed or upset, even minor setbacks can seem overwhelming, severely impacting overall productivity. Being aware of one's mood and its potential to sway focus and drive is essential for maintaining efficient day-to-day functioning.

A simple guideline to manage this is regular self-reflection. Through self-reflection, individuals become more attuned to their emotional responses. It encourages a healthier way of processing feelings, transforming negativity into constructive thoughts. By setting aside time for introspection, whether through journaling, meditation, or simply taking a moment to breathe, individuals develop a deeper understanding of their triggers and emotional patterns. This process not only helps in managing stress but also fosters resilience in the face of challenges, cultivating healthier emotional responses over time.

Increased self-awareness is another key element that profoundly impacts personal relationships. When individuals have a clear comprehension of their emotions, they communicate more effectively. They become better listeners, which is fundamental in any interaction. Self-aware people can empathize more easily because they understand their own feelings and, by extension, can relate to others' experiences. This understanding strengthens bonds with friends, family, and colleagues.

A practical approach to improving self-awareness involves seeking feedback and engaging in open dialogue with those around you. This doesn't mean becoming overly dependent on external opinions but rather using them as tools for growth. Feedback helps identify blind spots that might be affecting interpersonal dynamics. By practicing active listening and considering others' perspectives, individuals can adjust their behavior, resulting in more harmonious relationships.

It's important to recognize that while emotions are deeply personal, their effects extend beyond the individual. Emotional spillover occurs when one's emotional state influences others. For example, a team leader's positive energy and passion can inspire and motivate their team. On the other hand, a leader's stress and irritability may inadvertently create a tense atmosphere. Thus, being mindful of how emotions affect group dynamics is essential for fostering an environment that promotes collective success.

Moreover, understanding emotional awareness is particularly valuable for young professionals striving to build effective coping mechanisms amid workplace challenges. By developing emotional intelligence, they learn to navigate complex social landscapes, manage conflicts skillfully, and establish a supportive network. Emotional intelligence encompasses self-regulation, empathy, and social skills, all vital components that contribute to thriving in both professional and personal endeavors.

One strategy for enhancing emotional awareness is through mindfulness practices. Mindfulness encourages present-moment awareness, helping individuals observe and understand their emotions without judgment. Techniques such as meditation and deep breathing exercises are excellent ways to cultivate this awareness. These practices enable individuals to pause and reflect before reacting impulsively, ultimately improving emotional regulation.

Another tactic is embracing empathy. Practicing empathetic listening allows individuals to connect more deeply with others, promoting mutual understanding and reducing conflict. By acknowledging and valuing different perspectives, one not only fosters empathy but also broadens their emotional awareness, enhancing the quality of their relationships.

Furthermore, it's crucial to integrate self-care rituals into daily routines to maintain a healthy balance between emotional acuity and well-being. Engaging in activities that nourish the mind and body, such as exercise, creative pursuits, or spending time in nature, can help rejuvenate emotional resources and prevent burnout. Balancing emotional insights with self-care ensures that individuals remain grounded and resilient amidst life's demands.

Recognize the Signs of Emotional Turbulence

Understanding when emotions become unmanageable is a crucial skill for young adults navigating the path to adulthood. Emotions that spiral out of control can significantly impact one's life, often manifesting through various symptoms and behaviors. Recognizing these signals early can help in addressing emotional distress effectively.

Physical symptoms can often be the first indicator that your emotions might be getting out of hand. Fatigue is one of the most common signs, often overlooked as just being tired. However, persistent exhaustion can signal deeper emotional issues. Constantly feeling drained without any apparent reason might point toward underlying stress or depression. Another example is headaches, which are frequently tied to stress and anxiety. These physical manifestations should not be ignored, as they can serve as a wake-up call to assess your emotional well-being.

Moving beyond the physical, behavioral changes can provide

a clearer picture of emotional health. Withdrawal from social interactions, for instance, could suggest more profound issues. When you find yourself consistently avoiding friends and family or staying in your comfort zone rather than engaging with others, it's worth considering what might be driving this behavior. Isolation can exacerbate feelings of loneliness and sadness, creating a vicious cycle that's hard to break. At this point, it's crucial to recognize when withdrawal is not just a preference for solitude but an escape from dealing with emotional turmoil.

Changes in eating or sleeping patterns can also signal emotional dysregulation, acting as telltale signs that something may be amiss. For instance, someone experiencing anxiety might struggle with insomnia, as their mind races with endless worries at night. On the other hand, excessive sleeping can be indicative of depression, where fatigue and lack of motivation make waking up feel like an insurmountable task. Similarly, shifts in appetite—whether it's overeating as a form of comfort or losing interest in food altogether—can highlight emotional instability. It's essential to pay attention to these changes, as they often reflect how an individual copes with stress and emotional challenges.

Persistent negative thinking represents another significant hurdle in managing emotions. Thoughts heavily skewed towards negativity can magnify emotional difficulties, making everyday tasks seem overwhelming. This kind of thinking often leads to a downward spiral where pessimism breeds more negativity, affecting one's outlook on life and self-worth. For young adults grappling with new responsibilities and pressures, it becomes vital to address this mindset. Engaging in positive self-talk or seeking professional guidance can provide tools to challenge and change these thought patterns.

Understanding these signs and behaviors is only part of the journey towards better emotional management. Implementing practical strategies is equally important. For instance, establishing a routine can offer structure and stability, helping to manage changes in sleeping and eating patterns. Regular exercise and meditation have also been shown to positively affect both physical and emotional well-being by reducing stress levels and enhancing mood.

Developing a support network is another essential step. Connecting with friends, family, or mental health professionals provides a space to share experiences and gain perspective. Social support acts as a buffer against stress, offering reassurance and understanding when emotions threaten to become unmanageable. Sometimes, discussing feelings with those we trust can reveal insights and solutions we might not uncover alone.

For cognitive indicators such as negative thinking, techniques like cognitive-behavioral therapy (CBT) can prove beneficial. CBT focuses on identifying and challenging distorted thoughts, aiming to replace them with healthier, more balanced perspectives. This method empowers individuals to take control of their thoughts, reducing the impact of negativity on their emotions.

Lastly, awareness and education about mental health can equip young adults with the tools they need to identify and address emotional distress early. By familiarizing themselves with the warning signs and learning to recognize patterns in their own behavior and thoughts, they gain the ability to act proactively. Being informed about mental health fosters resilience and prepares young adults to face emotional challenges head-on, promoting a healthier and more balanced life.

Identify Stressors Specific to Young Adulthood

Recognizing the unique stressors during developmental stages is a critical aspect of understanding mental health and emotional intelligence. As young adults navigate the complexities of entering adulthood, they encounter various challenges that can lead to significant stress. One primary source of stress arises from transitioning through major life changes. Whether it's moving from high school to college, starting a new job, or shifting from dependency on parents to living independently, these transitions are loaded with uncertainty. They often require individuals to adapt quickly to new environments and expectations, which can be overwhelming.

During these transitional phases, the lack of familiarity and fear of the unknown can be particularly daunting. It's common to feel anxious about whether you'll fit in, meet academic or work-related expectations, or handle increased responsibilities effectively. To mitigate this anxiety, one practical guideline is preparation and planning. By anticipating potential challenges and developing strategies to address them, young adults can reduce feelings of uncertainty. For example, researching what to expect at a new job or creating a schedule for managing time more efficiently in college can provide a sense of control and confidence.

Evolving relationships also significantly contribute to the emotional strain experienced during these years. As friendships and familial bonds transform, and romantic relationships develop, there's an added layer of complexity in navigating social dynamics. The transition from adolescence to adulthood involves redefining these relationships, which can be emotionally taxing. Miscommunication and differing expectations often lead to conflicts, heightening emotional stress. Establishing clear communication channels and setting boundaries can be helpful guidelines to manage these evolving dynamics. Practicing open dialogue and expressing feelings honestly can foster healthier relationships, reducing emotional strain.

Financial pressures are another prominent stressor for emerging adults. Many face the daunting reality of student loans, credit card debts, or the challenge of budgeting with limited income. As financial independence becomes necessary, the burden of managing finances can be immense, contributing to heightened stress levels. Developing a practical approach to handling finances is crucial. Creating a budget, seeking financial literacy resources, or consulting a financial advisor can alleviate some of this pressure. Planning for future expenses and practicing disciplined saving habits can lead to better financial stability and reduced stress.

Young adults with chronic diseases or disabilities encounter additional layers of stress amid these transitions. Disease management and coping with limitations in opportunities add extra hurdles in their path towards development. According to Wood et al. (2017), successful navigation of such challenges requires substantial support systems tailored to individual needs. Ensuring access to suitable educational programs or health care services tailored to these individuals' requirements can enhance their developmental trajectory.

However, transitions aren't solely negative experiences. They offer opportunities for growth and self-discovery. Recognizing these opportunities is essential for building resilience. When young adults perceive change as a chance to learn and develop new skills, rather than solely a source of stress, they cultivate a more positive outlook. Embracing change and developing coping mechanisms, such as mindfulness practices or seeking mentorship, can further aid in managing transition-related stress.

It's vital for young adults to acknowledge that while the stressors they face are challenging, they are not insurmountable. Building effective coping mechanisms is key to managing these stresses and leading a balanced life. Emotional regulation techniques, like mindfulness or journaling, can help process emotions constructively. Establishing routines and prioritizing self-care activities, such as regular exercise or engaging in hobbies, enhances overall well-being.

Assess Your Current Emotional Intelligence Level

Embarking on the journey to evaluate and enhance emotional intelligence can be transformative for young adults. Emotional intelligence, or EI, is not just about understanding your emotions but also managing them effectively and empathizing with others. Here's how you can practically evaluate and work on boosting your emotional intelligence.

Self-Assessment Tools

The first step towards evaluating emotional intelligence is through self-assessment. You can utilize tools like questionnaires and quizzes designed to measure different aspects of emotional intelligence, such as empathy, self-awareness, and emotional regulation. These tools often highlight your strengths and weaknesses, providing a clear picture of where you stand. For instance, if a questionnaire reveals that managing stress is your weak point, it signals an area needing attention. Regularly engaging with these tools helps track progress over time, offering insights into how your emotional intelligence evolves.

Reflection Exercises

Reflection exercises are another crucial method to analyze emotional reactions. Since emotions can sometimes feel overwhelming or confusing, reflecting on them through activities like journaling allows you to dissect your feelings calmly. Set aside dedicated time each day to jot down thoughts and feelings. Consistency, such as journaling before bed or practicing mindfulness in the morning, can make self-reflection a habit. Engaging in mindfulness practices not only calms the mind but also sharpens awareness of your emotional state, helping you understand triggers and patterns. Such reflective practices create the space needed to process experiences healthily, promoting self-growth and self-discovery.

Setting Goals

Setting goals plays a pivotal role in fostering growth in emotional capabilities. Once self-assessment and reflection clarify areas for improvement, it's essential to set realistic and achievable goals. These might include learning techniques to better communicate emotions or strategies to improve empathetic listening. It's beneficial to break these goals into smaller, manageable tasks. For example, if enhancing empathy is your target, start by practicing active listening in everyday conversations. Goal-setting encourages continuous development, moving you closer to becoming emotionally adept. As with any skill-building, patience and perseverance are key. Celebrate small victories along your journey to maintain motivation.

Ongoing Learning and Adaptation

Emotional intelligence is not a static trait; it requires ongoing learning and adaptation. Engaging in workshops, reading books on emotional intelligence, and participating in group discussions can offer fresh perspectives and new strategies. Every interaction provides a learning opportunity—observe your responses during challenging situations and consciously apply improved emotional strategies next time. Being open to change and adapting to feedback from others can significantly boost emotional growth. Furthermore, understanding that setbacks are part of the learning curve is vital. Instead of viewing challenges as failures, see them as opportunities to refine emotional skills, thus fostering resilience.

Bringing It All Together

As we've explored these topics, it's clear that understanding mental health and emotional intelligence can truly empower young adults. By learning the key terms and recognizing signs of emotional turbulence, individuals gain the ability to articulate their feelings and experiences more effectively. This chapter has shed light on how such awareness not only benefits personal well-being but also helps in fostering stronger relationships with friends, family, and even colleagues. With this knowledge, young adults become better equipped to navigate the emotional ups and downs of life, making informed decisions about when to seek help and how to manage stress.

Moreover, embracing the tools for self-assessment and reflection discussed here can lead to meaningful growth. These practices lay a foundation for managing emotions in a healthy way and improving interpersonal skills. Whether you're a college student juggling studies and social life or a professional looking to build resilience at work, cultivating emotional intelligence offers numerous advantages. It's by understanding and nurturing these aspects of our mental health that we can truly thrive in both personal and professional settings. Remember, being proactive in this journey paves the way for a balanced and fulfilling lifestyle.

3

Daily Habits for a Happier Mind

Daily Habits to Uplift Your Mood and Create Positivity

U plifting your mood and fostering positivity are powerful goals to embrace as part of your daily routine. From the moment you wake up until you close your eyes at night, small habits can significantly influence how you perceive and respond to the world around you. Imagine starting each day with a mindset ready to welcome joy and optimism, setting the tone not only for how you handle challenges but also for how you celebrate successes. This chapter focuses on the transformative power of integrating these uplifting practices into daily life, steering away from negativity and towards a more fulfilling existence.

In this chapter, you'll explore several practical habits designed to enhance your mood and invite positivity into your everyday experiences. It begins with the impactful practice of gratitude journaling, where recognizing small joys becomes a cornerstone of happiness. You'll learn about crafting and reciting positive affirmations, which can reshape self-perception and fortify mental resilience. The benefits of physical activity are highlighted, showcasing how movement can function as both a stress reliever and a mood enhancer. You'll also be introduced to the value of dedicating time to hobbies and creative pursuits that offer an escape and boost emotional well-being. Lastly, the chapter discusses the importance of managing social media consumption to clear mental clutter and foster real-world connections. These diverse approaches come together to equip you with tools for cultivating a vibrant, positive lifestyle tailored to meet the unique stressors faced by young adults, college students, and young professionals today.

Start Your Day with a Gratitude Journal Entry

Understanding the ability of gratitude to shift our mental focus toward positivity can have profound effects on our daily lives. Engaging in the practice of gratitude is more than just saying "thank you." It's about recognizing and appreciating what we have, which leads to increased happiness levels and an overall sense of well-being.

Research demonstrates that regularly expressing gratitude can lead to higher levels of happiness. Studies conducted by Dr. Robert A. Emmons from the University of California and Dr. Michael E. McCullough from the University of Miami illustrate this relationship. In one experiment, participants who took time each week to write down things they were grateful for experienced a noticeable increase in optimism and felt better about their lives compared to those who focused on negative or neutral experiences (Harvard Health Publishing, 2021). This act of recognition helps shift our attention away from what we lack and redirects it to what we already possess, effectively nurturing a positive mindset.

A crucial component of this practice is journaling about gratitude. Maintaining a consistent habit of jotting down things that we are thankful for can significantly enhance emotional well-being. By doing so, individuals take an active step in consciously acknowledging the positive experiences and influences in their lives, which often go unnoticed amid the hustle of everyday life. Journaling not only provides a physical space to capture these moments but also serves as a tangible reminder of positivity during challenging times. For instance, reflecting on past entries during a rough patch reveals a pattern of goodness that boosts morale and mentally prepares us to handle adversity.

The art of gratitude journaling involves more than just listing items; it's about diving into the specifics of why something made you feel grateful. This depth encourages mindfulness, allowing you to savor small yet significant pleasures. Perhaps it's the smell of fresh coffee on a busy morning or a random compliment from a stranger. Taking the time to recognize these moments fosters a deeper appreciation for the nuances in life, contributing to a heightened state of contentment and peace.

Moreover, gratitude enhances resilience by shifting focus from negativity. Life, as we know, is fraught with challenges and setbacks, and it's easy to become ensnared in cycles of pessimism and anxiety. However, gratitude acts as a powerful antidote to this negativity. When we focus on what is going right in our lives, we cultivate an internal environment resilient to external disruptions. This doesn't mean ignoring problems, but rather approaching them with a fortified mental strength derived from understanding and appreciating life's positives.

When we consistently practice gratitude, we also open ourselves up to forming stronger social bonds. Gratitude encourages us to acknowledge the roles others play in our successes and happiness. Whether it's a supportive friend or a mentor who's guided us through tough times, expressing appreciation strengthens these relationships. According to research, showing gratitude in personal interactions — like thanking a partner or colleague — not only improves the dynamic of the relationship but also boosts self-esteem and confidence in that interaction's context (Datu et al., 2021).

Further supporting this notion, studies reveal that engaging in gratitude practices can lead to healthier lifestyle choices and reduced visits to healthcare providers, illustrating its holistic impact. A study involving workplace contexts showed that simply expressing thanks to employees led to increased productivity and satisfaction (Harvard Health Publishing, 2021). This ripple effect underscores how gratitude contributes to a well-rounded sense of fulfillment, impacting not only personal attitudes but also work ethics and achievements.

Despite some mixed findings in specific populations like children or middle-aged women (Harvard Health Publishing, 2021), the overarching evidence remains strong for most demographics. Gratitude has established itself as a key contributor to personal happiness and interpersonal success, making it a valuable tool in any young adult's emotional arsenal.

Incorporating gratitude into daily life doesn't have to be overwhelming or complicated. Simple actions, such as writing thank-you notes, mentally acknowledging appreciation without needing to express it out loud, or even counting your blessings weekly, can have profound effects. These practices encourage reflection on positive experiences, helping to implant an optimistic outlook that naturally wards off negativity.

Practice Positive Affirmations Each Morning

Optimism can be a powerful tool in reshaping self-perception, fostering a brighter outlook on life. At the heart of this transformation are positive affirmations, which serve as a shield against negative thoughts and an ally in boosting self-love. Imagine starting each day with a set of uplifting statements that counteract the nagging doubts and insecurities we all face. These affirmations remind us of our worth, help maintain emotional balance, and cultivate a sense of inner peace.

To harness the full potential of positive affirmations, it's essential to create specific ones tailored to individual needs and aspirations. Generic affirmations may provide some comfort, but personalized declarations resonate deeper, reinforcing personal growth and confidence. For instance, instead of merely stating, "I am happy," consider the more targeted approach of "I embrace challenges as opportunities for growth." This specificity aligns with personal values and goals, making the affirmation more impactful and leading to genuine self-improvement over time.

Incorporating these affirmations into a daily morning routine can significantly enhance their effectiveness. Mornings offer a fresh start, and beginning your day by reaffirming positive beliefs sets the tone for everything that follows. Much like brushing your teeth or having breakfast, integrating affirmations into this routine makes positivity a natural part of your life. Start small, perhaps by reciting three affirmations while getting ready for the day. Over time, this practice not only becomes second nature but also an anchor amidst life's chaos, helping to maintain focus and motivation when you need it most.

Studies have shown that self-affirmation practices can influence neural pathways, particularly those related to self-worth and value processing (Cascio et al., 2016). Engaging in positive affirmations activates brain regions such as the ventromedial prefrontal cortex, which plays a crucial role in how we evaluate ourselves and our experiences (Falk et al., 2015; Cascio et al., 2016). By regularly affirming personal values and achievements, you're essentially training your brain to view yourself in a more favorable light, which can lead to a more resilient and optimistic mindset.

Furthermore, self-affirmations can decrease stress levels and improve overall well-being (Sherman et al., 2009; Critcher & Dunning, 2015). In moments of doubt or anxiety, recalling your affirmations can serve as a mental refuge, providing reassurance and clarity. They remind you of your strengths, capabilities, and the unique qualities that define you. This is particularly beneficial for young adults and professionals facing various pressures from school, work, and relationships. By equipping yourself with a toolkit of positive affirmations, you're better prepared to handle life's challenges with grace and confidence.

Creating affirmations requires some reflection. Begin by identifying areas in your life where you'd like to see change or improvement. What are the negative thoughts that often occupy your mind? Once you've pinpointed these areas, craft statements that directly counter those thoughts. If you find yourself frequently doubting your abilities, try an affirmation like "I have the skills and determination to achieve my goals" or "Every challenge I face is a step toward success."

It's also helpful to ensure that your affirmations are framed positively, focusing on what you want rather than what you wish to avoid. For example, instead of saying, "I will not be anxious," say, "I am calm and in control." Words hold power, and using language that emphasizes positivity aids in cultivating a more optimistic perspective.

The process of creating affirmations doesn't have to be solitary—consider sharing them with a friend or family member who can support your journey. Discussing your goals and the affirmations that accompany them can foster accountability and encouragement, further strengthening the practice.

Remember, consistency is key. Like any habit, the impact of affirmations builds over time. Commit to your chosen affirmations, revisiting and adjusting them as needed to keep them relevant to your evolving aspirations.

Ultimately, the journey of reshaping self-perception through optimism and affirmations is deeply personal. It requires patience, introspection, and a willingness to embrace change. Yet, the rewards—a more positive self-image, increased resilience, and enhanced well-being—are undeniably worthwhile.

Incorporate Physical Activity into Your Routine

Physical activity holds a significant role in boosting mood and fostering positivity, serving as both a natural stress reliever and a morale booster. At the core of this phenomenon is exercise's ability to release endorphins, which are chemicals in the brain that act as natural painkillers and mood elevators. Engaging in physical activities, such as running, cycling, or even walking briskly, prompts the brain to release these endorphins. This rush of endorphins can help reduce stress, combat anxiety, and provide an overall sense of well-being that can last long after the workout ends.

Finding enjoyment in the activities you choose is key to maintaining motivation for regular exercise. The idea isn't just about enduring exercise but finding movement that feels less like a chore and more like something you look forward to. Some people thrive in the structured environment of a gym, sweating it out on machines or lifting weights. Others might find joy in the rhythm of a dance class, the peaceful stretch of yoga, or the camaraderie found in team sports. Even activities like hiking or playing frisbee can be great options if they resonate with your interests. The important thing is to experiment until you discover what you genuinely enjoy. Enjoyment not only makes the activity itself more pleasurable but also serves as a powerful motivator to keep coming back, making exercise a sustainable habit rather than a fleeting resolution.

Incorporating exercise into your daily routine requires strategic thinking, especially amidst busy schedules. One practical approach is integrating short bursts of activity into your day. This can be as simple as taking quick 10-minute walks during breaks at work or school, or doing brief sets of exercises like squats or pushups at home. These small increments can add up significantly, contributing to improved mood and better health over time without demanding large blocks of your schedule. Consistency is essential; regular movement, no matter how small, reinforces the behavior until it becomes second nature.

Another effective strategy for embedding physical activity into daily life is socializing your fitness routine. Exercising with friends, family, or colleagues not only adds a layer of accountability but also increases the fun factor. Planning regular meet-ups for walks, jogs, or group classes can transform exercise from a solitary task to a social event. This means you're more likely to stick with it because there's a communal aspect that's both enjoyable and supportive. People often think of working out as an individual challenge, but it doesn't have to be. A shared experience can make all the difference, turning an isolated endeavor into a bonding opportunity that strengthens both your body and your relationships (Mayo Clinic, 2022).

It's essential to remember that variety is the spice of life when it comes to exercise. If you've been doing the same workout for months, you might find your enthusiasm waning. Mixing things up by trying new activities can reignite your interest, keep things fresh, and prevent boredom. Additionally, different forms of exercise can offer varying benefits; while running is excellent for cardiovascular health, incorporating strength training can build muscle, and stretching exercises like yoga or Pilates improve flexibility and relieve stress. Each type of exercise brings its own set of benefits to your mental and physical health, so rotating between them can create a well-rounded fitness regime that supports overall well-being.

Finally, it's crucial to frame physical activity not as another obligation on your to-do list but as an integral part of your self-care routine. By perceiving exercise as a gift you give yourself—a vital component of managing stress and enhancing your mood—you cultivate a mindset that appreciates and prioritizes physical activity. Whether you're engaging in a high-intensity interval training session or enjoying a meditative walk through a local park, recognize that each step, jump, or stretch you take contributes to a healthier, happier you (Robinson et al., 2018).

Dedicate Time to a Hobby or Creative Pursuit

Engaging in hobbies can be a transformative journey that brings stress relief and avenues for self-expression into your daily life. It's not just about engaging in activities to pass the time; it's about finding fulfillment and a sense of peace amidst the chaos of everyday responsibilities. The power of hobbies lies in their ability to provide an escape, a space where you can immerse yourself in something purely enjoyable and enriching. For young adults and college students juggling academic demands or young professionals facing workplace challenges, incorporating hobbies into daily routines can offer essential mental health benefits.

First and foremost, hobbies play a crucial role in stress management. When you engage in an activity you love, whether it's painting, gardening, hiking, or playing a musical instrument, your mind shifts focus. This shift acts like a mental cleanse, pulling you away from sources of stress and allowing you to recharge both mentally and emotionally. Studies have shown that people who regularly engage in leisure activities report better mood, reduced stress levels, and greater life satisfaction (Lagunes-Córdoba et al., 2022). This is because hobbies often involve creativity, sensory engagement, and relaxation, which are integral to maintaining good mental health and well-being.

Picking the right hobby involves exploring what truly excites you. It's essential to choose activities that resonate with your interests and passions. Think about what makes you happy. Do you find peace in nature? Perhaps hiking or gardening would suit you. Are you drawn to creativity? Consider trying out painting, writing, or photography. The key is to experiment with different activities until you discover what sparks joy and excitement. This process of exploration is not only fun but can also lead to new discoveries about yourself and your capabilities, fostering self-expression and personal growth.

For those struggling to find the time to indulge in hobbies, prioritization and structured scheduling are vital. In our busy lives, it's easy to overlook leisure activities. However, making time for hobbies is an investment in your mental and emotional well-being. Start by analyzing your daily schedule and identifying time slots that can be dedicated to your hobby. This doesn't mean you need to devote hours on end; even dedicating 15-30 minutes each day can make a significant difference. Establishing a routine helps incorporate these activities seamlessly into your lifestyle, ensuring they become a consistent source of enjoyment and relaxation.

Moreover, taking part in hobby groups or clubs can enhance social connections, further contributing to stress relief. Being part of a community with shared interests fosters a sense of belonging and reduces feelings of loneliness and isolation—a common challenge faced by many young adults today. Whether it's joining a book club, participating in a local sports team, or attending art classes, these social engagements enrich your experience and broaden your network of support.

The benefits of engaging in hobbies are numerous and well-documented (Godman, 2024). Hobbies not only distract you from everyday stresses but also contribute positively to your overall happiness and satisfaction. They provide a platform for self-expression, allowing you to communicate thoughts and emotions through various creative outlets. For many, this form of expression becomes an important aspect of their identity, helping to build confidence and resilience.

Limit Social Media Consumption for Mental Clarity

In the digital age, social media has become a ubiquitous part of daily life, bridging distances and keeping us connected. However, as with any powerful tool, its excessive use can have unintended consequences, particularly on mental health. Let's explore the negative effects of spending too much time scrolling through feeds and why it's essential to cultivate mindful habits around social media usage.

One significant impact of excessive social media use is the rise in anxiety levels among users. The constant barrage of curated images and updates often leads to the phenomenon known as "comparison culture." When individuals see carefully selected snapshots of others' seemingly perfect lives, it can trigger feelings of inadequacy and self-doubt. This comparison isn't just about looks but extends to lifestyle and achievements, creating an unrealistic standard that can leave many users feeling like they never quite measure up.

Further compounding this issue is the link between excessive social media use and diminished self-esteem. The focus on likes, comments, and shares can turn postings into popularity contests, where people begin to equate their worth with online validation. As users chase these metrics, they might find themselves posting content that doesn't authentically represent them, eroding their sense of self-worth. Over time, this constant need for approval can lead to severe dips in self-esteem and contribute to a cycle of negative self-perception.

To combat these adverse effects, setting boundaries around social media usage is crucial. By consciously moderating the amount and type of content consumed, individuals can regain control over their online experiences. This might include establishing specific times of the day dedicated to checking social media or implementing daily limits on screen time. Additionally, being selective about which accounts to follow is another effective way to mitigate negativity; unfollowing accounts that don't inspire positivity can significantly enhance one's online environment.

Moreover, taking breaks from screens altogether allows for a richer engagement with the world beyond pixels. Instead of defaulting to social media during downtime, exploring alternative activities offers fulfilling ways to spend free time. Engaging in offline activities such as reading, drawing, hiking, or even cooking can boost creativity and provide a break from relentless digital stimuli. These activities not only enrich leisure time but also foster real-world connections, encouraging individuals to interact more deeply with those around them.

The importance of face-to-face interactions cannot be overstated as they offer emotional depth that virtual connections often lack. Initiating conversation with friends or attending community events are great ways to counteract the isolation that may come with heavy social media reliance. These interactions provide opportunities for genuine connection and support, critical elements often missing in online exchanges.

Furthermore, the benefits of curating a balanced digital life extend beyond personal well-being. For young professionals, managing social media use efficiently can translate into improved productivity and workplace satisfaction. Reducing distraction by limiting social media interactions during work hours can lead to more focused and efficient work patterns, enhancing overall performance and career prospects.

By recognizing these negative traits and actively choosing to implement healthier practices, individuals are better positioned to enjoy the benefits of social media without falling prey to its detrimental effects. Moving forward, one strategy to uphold these changes could be aligning social media habits with personal values and goals. For instance, if someone values learning, they might prioritize following educational channels or joining groups that share informative content. This intentional selection helps transform social media from a source of anxiety into a platform for growth and inspiration.

Bringing It All Together

As you reflect on the ideas shared in this chapter, think about how establishing daily habits can genuinely uplift your mood and bring positivity into your life. Starting with a gratitude journal offers a powerful shift in perspective, allowing you to focus on what's working well rather than what's not. By jotting down what you're thankful for, you foster an appreciation for the everyday blessings that often go unnoticed. Positive affirmations further strengthen this positive mindset. They remind you of your worth and potential each morning, setting a hopeful tone for your day. Tailoring these affirmations to fit your personal goals can make them even more impactful, promoting genuine self-esteem and resilience.

Physical activity complements these practices by naturally boosting your mood with endorphins while also providing a stress-relieving outlet. Choosing activities that bring joy ensures that exercise is sustainable and enjoyable. Engaging in hobbies or creative pursuits taps into your passions, offering re-laxation and a break from daily stresses. Limiting social media consumption helps maintain mental clarity, reducing anxiety and fostering real-world connections. Together, these habits form a supportive framework for navigating life's challenges, empowering you to lead a fulfilling and balanced lifestyle.

4

Mastering Mindfulness

Mindfulness for Young Adults: Cultivating Inner Peace

Mindfulness for young adults is a gateway to tranquility in an often hectic world. Imagine the feeling of being truly present, fully engaging with the here and now without the mental clutter of past regrets or future worries. This chapter invites young adults to embark on a journey toward inner peace through mindfulness practices tailored specifically for them. It's about cultivating moments of calmness and clarity amidst the busyness of life that many young people navigate in school, work, and relationships. This soothing practice can be compared to finding a quiet room within oneself, where serenity reigns and distractions fade away.

Throughout this chapter, you'll discover practical techniques designed to reduce anxiety and instill a sense of calmness. We'll delve into mindfulness practices like mindful breathing and meditation, revealing how these tools can transform everyday experiences and foster emotional resilience. You'll learn about the power of non-judgmental observation, enabling you to approach thoughts and feelings with acceptance rather than criticism. By exploring different mindful activities such as breath awareness and eating mindfully, we aim to equip young adults with strategies to enhance focus and embrace a balanced lifestyle. Whether you're a college student trying to balance studies and social life or a young professional seeking effective coping mechanisms at work, these exercises will help guide you toward a more peaceful, fulfilling life. As you read on, prepare to unlock the potential of mindfulness in your daily routine, crafting a refuge of calm amid life's bustling demands.

Principles of Mindfulness Meditation

Mindfulness for young adults is like a breath of fresh air amid the chaos of modern life. It encourages us to pause and simply be present, which is both a simple yet powerful concept. Imagine you're standing on a beach, focusing not on the worries about tomorrow's tasks or yesterday's regrets but on the sound of waves and the warm sand beneath your feet. This is mindfulness—an invitation to fully engage with the present moment.

At its core, mindfulness is about awareness. It's about breaking away from our routine of constantly projecting into the future or dwelling on the past. When practiced regularly, mindfulness can act as a balm for the mind, providing relief from the endless loop of thoughts that often leads to stress or unhappiness. Harvard research suggests that we spend almost half of our waking hours thinking about something other than what we're doing, often resulting in decreased happiness. Mindfulness helps redirect this wandering attention to the here and now, fostering a sense of peace and satisfaction in everyday experiences.

An essential aspect of mindfulness is non-judgmental observation. This practice encourages individuals to view their thoughts and feelings without labeling them as good or bad. By cultivating this form of observation, one can develop greater self-acceptance and awareness of negative thought patterns that contribute to anxiety. For instance, if a student receives a poor grade, rather than spiraling into self-criticism ("I'm not good enough"), practicing non-judgmental awareness allows them to acknowledge the disappointment without further judgment, paving the way for constructive thinking.

This approach can also help dismantle entrenched beliefs that quietly fuel anxiety and low self-esteem. By observing our thoughts without bias, we learn to understand rather than suppress them, leading to healthier emotional responses. Such self-acceptance is critical for young adults who are often bombarded by societal pressures and expectations. Instead of seeing setbacks as failures, they become opportunities for growth and understanding.

Practices such as focusing on breath serve as vital components of meditation. The breath acts as an anchor that grounds the individual, linking the mind and body in moments of stillness. In meditation classes, the common instruction to "return to the breath" highlights how this simple act can calm the nervous system and promote relaxation. Scientific studies back this up, demonstrating that mindful breathing can decrease the production of cortisol, a stress hormone, thus enhancing emotional resilience.

Breath awareness doesn't just start and end in meditation sessions—it's a tool that can be integrated throughout daily life. Whether it's taking deep breaths before a challenging conversation or using breathwork during periods of intense concentration at work or study, this practice helps maintain composure and focus. For college students juggling exams and social life, learning to harness the breath can transform stressful days into manageable ones.

Understanding different meditation techniques can further personalize mindfulness practices. Techniques such as body scans, where one brings conscious attention to various parts of the body, can particularly benefit those who struggle to quiet their minds through traditional sittings. Body scans offer a structured method to promote relaxation and reduce tension. By paying deliberate attention from head to toe, individuals can recognize areas where stress is held and consciously release it.

Meditation is not a one-size-fits-all journey. Some may find walking meditations—focusing on each step and the sensation of moving—to be more suited to their preferences. Others might prefer guided visualizations that use imagery to evoke a state of calm. By exploring different approaches, young adults can tailor mindfulness practices to fit their personal needs and lifestyles.

It's crucial to remember that while mindfulness offers many benefits aimed at improving mental well-being, it does require commitment and patience. Much like learning any new skill, consistency plays a significant role. Regular practice—even if it's just a few minutes each day—can gradually lead to profound shifts in one's outlook and emotional health.

There is indeed solid empirical support suggesting mindfulness' positive implications for psychological health (Keng et al.,

2011). Mindfulness-based interventions have shown efficacy in reducing symptoms of anxiety and depression, making them appealing options for young adults navigating life's challenges (Hofmann & Gómez, 2017).

Integrating mindfulness into one's life provides tools for transforming reactive behaviors into reflective ones. For young professionals, it means approaching workplace challenges with a balanced mindset, ready to adapt rather than react impulsively. For college students, mindfulness becomes a companion guiding them through academic pressures with greater clarity and poise.

Integrating Mindful Breathing Exercises

The journey into mindfulness often begins with something as fundamental as breathing. When life feels overwhelming, turning to simple breath-awareness techniques can ground individuals in moments of anxiety or stress. This practice is about focusing on each breath and bringing attention back to it whenever the mind wanders. It's a way to reclaim control and foster a sense of calm amid chaos.

Imagine being caught in a whirlwind of thoughts about assignments, meetings, or personal challenges. Simple breath awareness offers an anchor, a way to return to the present moment. By inhaling deeply and exhaling slowly, young adults can find a peaceful refuge within themselves. Each breath acts as a reminder that not everything demands immediate reaction; some things are best approached from a state of calm.

Beyond basic breath awareness lies the 4-7-8 breathing technique, a structured method offering deeper relaxation, which is widely celebrated for its benefits. This method involves inhaling through the nose for four seconds, holding the breath for seven seconds, and exhaling through the mouth for eight seconds. Regularly practicing this technique can significantly aid sleep quality, alleviate stress, and improve the overall state of well-being (Winnipeg, 2024).

Many find the 4-7-8 method to be transformative, particularly before bedtime or during high-stress situations. It serves as a mental reset button, facilitating a smoother transition into sleep by calming racing thoughts and steadying the mind. In a fast-paced world, this routine can become a cherished moment of tranquility amidst daily pressures.

For those who wonder how to seamlessly integrate mindfulness into their lives without dedicating hours to practice, combining mindful breathing with daily activities can be highly effective. Consider everyday tasks like walking to classes, making breakfast, or even waiting in line. These moments, typically overlooked, present opportunities to connect breath with action. Imagine the rhythm of your footsteps aligning with the cadence of your breath. This synergy doesn't require extra time; it simply requires intention and awareness.

Mindful eating is another fantastic example. By paying attention to each bite, savoring flavors, and feeling textures, meals evolve from mere consumption into experiences of presence and gratitude. As you engage in such practices, you'll likely discover an enhanced enjoyment of life's simpler moments, cultivating a fuller appreciation for the present.

However, establishing any new habit requires reminders, especially when starting out. Setting consistent reminders for mindful breathing can introduce these practices into the daily routine. These cues might be phone alerts, sticky notes, or associating breathing exercises with regular events, like brushing teeth or setting the morning alarm. Such reminders foster emotional resilience through the development of positive habits.

Think of these reminders as gentle nudges toward self-care. They serve as checkpoints throughout the day—a call to pause and breathe, to reconnect with oneself. This habitual engagement nurtures a greater capacity to handle stressful situations as they arise. Over time, you may notice a natural inclination towards mindfulness, even without needing external prompts.

As these breathing techniques and integration strategies cultivate mindfulness and inner peace, they also build essential skills for managing life's hurdles. Whether facing academic deadlines, navigating relationship dynamics, or addressing workplace pressures, the tools gained through mindful breathing empower individuals to respond rather than react. They nurture clarity and composure, forming a resilient mindset that remains grounded.

Being Present in Everyday Tasks

Incorporating mindfulness into daily activities can significantly enhance focus and enjoyment, providing a sense of peace amidst the busyness of life. By cultivating mindfulness in routine tasks, young adults can transform mundane actions into opportunities for growth and awareness. Let's explore how mindful walking, eating, conversing, and household chores can enrich our lives.

Imagine taking a stroll where each step connects you to your surroundings, creating a peaceful rhythm that soothes your mind. Mindful walking is about engaging fully with the environment. It's not just about moving from one place to another but noticing the subtle textures underfoot, the rustle of leaves, or the gentle breeze on your skin. When practiced regularly, this form of walking fosters a profound appreciation for simple moments. It encourages you to pause and breathe, leaving stress behind as you ground yourself in the present. To get started, choose a path you enjoy, whether it's a garden, park, or even your neighborhood. As you walk, gently direct your attention to your senses: what you see, hear, or feel. This practice transforms walking into a calming, joyful experience and enhances your connection with the world around you.

Similarly, mindful eating can revolutionize your relationship with food. In today's fast-paced world, meals often become quick, distracted affairs. Yet, eating with intention allows you to savor flavors and textures deeply. Imagine your favorite dish: its aroma, the burst of spice or sweetness with each bite. By focusing on these details, you create a rich sensory experience that enhances satisfaction and digestion. Studies suggest that mindfulness during meals can help manage eating habits and improve overall health. To practice, begin by taking a moment to appreciate your meal's appearance and aroma. Then, take small bites, chewing slowly and deliberately, without distractions like phones or television. With time, you'll find that mindful eating not only nourishes your body but also grants a moment of tranquility amidst the hustle and bustle.

Moving beyond individual practice, mindfulness can transform social interactions, fostering deeper connections. Engaging fully in conversations involves truly listening — not planning responses while others speak but absorbing their words with empathy and curiosity. This active listening nurtures mutual understanding and supports healthier relationships. Imagine a conversation where both parties feel heard and valued, leading to meaningful exchanges rather than superficial chit-chat. By practicing mindfulness in communication, you learn to notice non-verbal cues and emotions, which strengthens bonds with friends, family, and colleagues. Next time you're chatting with someone, put away your phone, maintain eye contact, and focus entirely on what they're saying. Respond thoughtfully, considering their perspective. In doing so, you contribute to a supportive and engaged dialogue, enhancing interpersonal connections.

Mindfulness isn't limited to walking or talking; it extends to everyday tasks such as household chores. Performing chores mindfully might seem paradoxical at first, but it can convert monotonous routines into opportunities for relaxation and meditation. Washing dishes, folding laundry, or tidying up can become acts of care, both for your space and yourself. As you engage in these activities, pay attention to the sensations — the warmth of water, the texture of fabrics. This practice shifts your focus from task completion to the process itself, making it less of a chore and more of a peaceful ritual. Consider setting a regular time to complete chores mindfully, allowing yourself to experience the calmness and fulfillment that comes with attentively caring for your living environment.

Establishing a Nightly Reflection Practice

Creating a nightly reflection practice can be immensely beneficial for young adults seeking to enhance self-awareness and process emotions effectively. This practice not only aids in articulating feelings but also facilitates the recognition of mood patterns, thereby offering insight into one's emotional landscape. Journaling serves as a valuable tool in this regard, allowing individuals to express their thoughts and emotions with honesty and clarity. By putting words to feelings, journaling can help break down complex emotions into manageable pieces, making them easier to understand and navigate.

Moreover, keeping a journal can reveal recurring themes and triggers that may otherwise go unnoticed. Over time, these recorded reflections can act as a map of one's emotional terrain, highlighting patterns that contribute to stress or anxiety. Recognizing these patterns is the first step toward addressing them, enabling individuals to develop more effective strategies for managing their emotions and responses. The act of journaling provides an opportunity for introspection, fostering a deeper understanding of oneself and promoting personal growth over time.

Incorporating gratitude into your nightly reflection further enhances its benefits by shifting focus away from daily stressors and towards positive aspects of life. Gratitude reflection involves acknowledging and appreciating the good things in your day, no matter how small they might seem. This practice can cultivate a sense of positivity and improve overall emotional well-being. Reflecting on what you are thankful for encourages a mindset that prioritizes appreciation over negativity, which can transform how you perceive daily events and challenges.

Gratitude reflection also has profound effects on mental health. Studies have shown that regularly practicing gratitude can increase levels of happiness and decrease symptoms of depression. When we focus on gratitude, we create an upward spiral of positive emotions, which can lead to increased resilience against adversity. For young adults navigating the complexities of school, work, and relationships, this shift in perspective can be particularly empowering, offering a buffer against the pressures and stresses of everyday life.

Setting intentions for the following day is another vital component of a nightly reflection practice. This involves envisioning how you would like tomorrow to unfold and establishing specific, achievable goals to guide your actions. By setting clear intentions, you provide yourself with a roadmap for the day ahead, enhancing your sense of purpose and direction. This practice not only fosters a productive mindset but also instills confidence in your ability to achieve your aspirations.

When you set intentions, it helps in organizing thoughts and priorities. For instance, if you're a college student preparing for exams, your intention might be to study for a set number of hours and take breaks when needed. For young professionals, intentions could revolve around tackling tasks at work while maintaining a healthy work-life balance. These intentions act as daily commitments to yourself, encouraging you to stay focused and motivated while reducing the likelihood of being overwhelmed by various responsibilities.

Additionally, setting intentions can have ripple effects beyond the immediate goal. As you become consistent in achieving small daily objectives, this practice boosts self-discipline and commitment. Successful completion of intended tasks builds momentum, leading to greater accomplishments over time. It also promotes a sense of satisfaction at day's end, knowing that you have taken meaningful steps toward your long-term goals.

While journaling, gratitude reflection, and intention-setting provide structure to nightly reflections, incorporating self-compassion plays a crucial role in fostering non-judgmental growth and emotional healing. Self-compassion involves treating yourself with kindness and understanding, especially during challenging times or when facing personal shortcomings. Many young adults struggle with harsh self-criticism or negative self-talk, which can exacerbate stress and hinder emotional development.

Self-compassion encourages individuals to view their experiences through a lens of empathy and patience. Instead of judging oneself harshly for mistakes or perceived failures, this approach invites a more forgiving attitude, recognizing that imperfection is part of the human experience. By adopting a compassionate stance toward oneself, individuals can nurture a supportive inner dialogue that promotes healing and resilience.

This kind of reflection reminds us that everyone encounters obstacles and that setbacks do not define our worth. For example, if you didn't meet all your intentions for the day, acknowledge the effort you put in and consider what adjustments could be made without self-reprimand. Celebrate small victories and recognize progress, however incremental it may seem. Emphasizing self-compassion in your reflections reinforces the idea that growth is an ongoing journey rather than a destination.

Utilizing Mindfulness Apps

As young adults navigate the challenges of entering adulthood, finding balance amidst work, school, and personal relationships can often feel overwhelming. This is where mindfulness comes into play, serving as a valuable tool to help cultivate inner peace and reduce anxiety. A great way for young adults to incorporate mindfulness into their daily routines is through mindfulness apps, which are specially designed to enhance practice and provide guidance tailored to individual needs.

One of the most popular meditation apps is Headspace, known for its user-friendly approach to teaching mindfulness and meditation. Headspace offers a variety of features that cater to different experience levels, making it a versatile choice whether you're a beginner or more advanced in your mindfulness journey. The app provides guided meditations, short courses, and even animations that explain the concepts behind mindfulness practices in a relatable manner. Some users find this visual aspect particularly engaging, as it allows them to grasp the principles of mindfulness easily.

Similarly, Calm is another highly recommended app for cultivating mindfulness. It offers an appealing interface with soothing sounds, sleep stories, and guided sessions that focus on various goals such as stress reduction, focus enhancement, and better sleep. Trying out features like daily "calm sessions" can be an excellent way to start your day with intention and presence. What makes these apps particularly beneficial is their adaptability; they allow you to choose meditation lengths and themes according to your mood or schedule, promoting flexibility and facilitating digital mindfulness practices even amidst a busy lifestyle.

Beyond basic features, exploring additional options within these apps can further enrich your mindfulness journey. For example, some apps offer specific modes tailored to particular situations—like calming music for stressful commutes or relaxing bedtime audio to lull you into a restful sleep. Harnessing these features can motivate continual engagement by introducing variety and new experiences, maintaining your interest over time.

Moreover, community features in mindfulness apps play a

crucial role in fostering accountability and creating a supportive network. Whether it's joining virtual meditation groups or interacting with forums within the app, connecting with others on similar journeys can provide encouragement and shared insights. This community aspect not only reinforces your commitment to regular practice but also reminds you that you're not alone in your search for mental clarity and peace.

Furthermore, many mindfulness apps integrate reminders into their functionality, aiding consistency and facilitating the incorporation of mindfulness practices into daily life. Most apps provide options to set notifications that remind you to take mindful breaks or engage in meditation sessions at scheduled times. Establishing these reminders helps embed mindfulness habits into your routine with minimal effort, ensuring consistency and making mindfulness an integral part of everyday activities.

When setting up a regular practice with app reminders, consider creating a simple guideline to maximize your experience. Begin by identifying the times of day when you're most likely to benefit from a mindfulness session—before embarking on a busy day, during lunch breaks, or winding down before bed. Use the app's reminder feature to prompt yourself at these intervals, gently integrating mindfulness without disrupting your schedule. Over time, you'll notice how these small, consistent moments of mindfulness contribute significantly to establishing lasting, positive habits.

Summary and Reflections

In this chapter, we delved into the heart of mindfulness practices, offering young adults practical tools for fostering inner peace and reducing anxiety. By focusing on simple yet profound techniques like breath awareness, body scans, and walking meditations, we've highlighted how these can be seamlessly integrated into daily life. The emphasis has been on understanding mindfulness as a journey towards self-acceptance and emotional resilience, all while acknowledging that different approaches suit different individuals. Whether it's through mindful breathing exercises or incorporating mindfulness into everyday activities, the goal is to remain present, breaking away from stress-inducing thought patterns.

We've also examined how mindfulness techniques benefit both personal well-being and social interactions, encouraging young adults to build connections with others while maintaining mental clarity. As you navigate life's demands—be it academic pressures or workplace challenges—these strategies offer a balanced approach to handling emotions and cultivating a composed mindset. Mindfulness isn't just about finding moments of calm; it's about creating a sustainable foundation for managing life's hurdles. As you continue exploring these practices, remember that the commitment to regular practice and patience with oneself are key to unlocking the lasting benefits of mindfulness in your journey.

5

Building Emotional Resilience

Building Emotional Resilience in Young Adults

Building emotional resilience in young adults is a vital part of their journey through life. As they navigate the ups and downs of school, work, and personal relationships, developing strategies to cope with stress and adversity becomes crucial. Without these skills, the challenges they face can seem overwhelming, impeding their progress and diminishing their well-being. By focusing on the development of emotional resilience, young people can safeguard their mental health and foster a more balanced, fulfilling lifestyle.

In this chapter, we will delve into a variety of strategies designed to bolster emotional resilience among young adults. We'll explore how distinguishing between healthy and unhealthy coping mechanisms plays a pivotal role in managing stress effectively. Young adults will learn to recognize patterns of behavior that either support or undermine their mental health, enabling them to choose healthier approaches. The chapter will also introduce the concept of creating a personal support network, emphasizing the importance of having reliable connections that provide encouragement during tough times. Additionally, readers will gain insights into reframing negative thoughts to build a more positive mindset and break down overwhelming tasks into smaller, manageable steps. By establishing boundaries to protect their energy, young adults can ensure that they remain focused on what truly matters. Each section of the chapter aims to equip readers with practical techniques and guidance, empowering them to tackle life's adversities with greater confidence and poise.

Distinguish between Healthy and Unhealthy Coping Mechanisms

Recognizing the difference between beneficial and harmful coping mechanisms is essential for young adults navigating the complexities of adulthood. By understanding these differences, individuals can make more informed choices that promote emotional resilience and overall well-being.

Healthy coping strategies offer sustainable relief from stress and adversity by turning towards positive outlets like exercise, social interactions, and creative pursuits. Exercise, for example, is not just about maintaining physical health; it also plays a significant role in mental wellness. Activities such as jogging or yoga release endorphins, which alleviate stress and enhance mood, creating a natural buffer against emotional distress. Similarly, engaging in social activities connects people with their support networks, providing a sense of belonging and reassurance that they are not alone in their struggles.

Creative activities, be it painting, writing, or playing an instrument, provide an emotional release that can be therapeutic, helping individuals process emotions in a constructive manner. These activities allow one to express feelings without words, offering insight and clarity into one's emotional state. The act of creation itself can be empowering, reinforcing a sense of accomplishment and control amid life's uncertainties.

In stark contrast, unhealthy coping mechanisms often lead to greater distress and dysfunction over time. Substance abuse, avoidance behaviors, and self-criticism are common pitfalls that may provide temporary relief but ultimately exacerbate emotional issues. Alcohol or drug use, for instance, might momentarily dull the pain but can quickly become destructive, leading to dependency or further emotional turmoil. Avoidance behaviors, such as procrastination or denial of problems, create a cycle where issues remain unresolved, gradually snowballing into bigger challenges that are harder to tackle later on.

Self-criticism is another detrimental habit, eroding self-esteem and fostering a negative self-image. This harsh internal dialogue can trap individuals in a loop of negativity, reducing their ability to handle stress effectively and making them more vulnerable to anxiety and depression. Recognizing these patterns is the first step towards breaking free from them.

One practical approach to understanding and reforming coping strategies is conducting a personal coping inventory. This involves assessing one's current habits to identify which methods are healthy and which are harmful. Keeping a journal or using a structured questionnaire can help illuminate these patterns, revealing both the frequency and effectiveness of different coping techniques. Highlighting these habits can provide valuable insights, aiding individuals in recognizing areas requiring change and improvement.

For many, consulting with a mental health professional offers vital guidance in refining coping strategies. Therapists or counselors are trained to help individuals explore their thoughts and emotions, offering evidence-based techniques to replace ineffective coping mechanisms with healthier alternatives. Cognitive-behavioral therapy (CBT), for instance, helps reframe negative thinking patterns, promoting adaptive responses to stressors. Through therapy, individuals can build a repertoire of skills tailored to their unique needs, enhancing their ability to face challenges with resilience and confidence.

It's important to note that consultation with professionals not only aids in developing personalized coping strategies but also provides a safe space for self-exploration. Regular sessions can foster a deeper understanding of one's emotional triggers, enabling proactive management of stress before it escalates. This ongoing support acts as a stabilizing force, underpinning efforts to maintain mental health.

Ultimately, cultivating emotional resilience involves commitment and patience. Encouraging healthier choices starts with acknowledging the need for change and consistently working towards better coping mechanisms. By prioritizing positive outlets, identifying maladaptive behaviors, and seeking professional guidance, young adults can strengthen their emotional resilience. Over time, these efforts will translate into an improved capacity to navigate life's adversities, paving the way for a more balanced and fulfilling future.

Create a Personal Support Network

Building emotional resilience in young adults involves creating supportive networks that provide essential emotional support, guidance, and encouragement. Establishing these connections is foundational for managing stress and adversity, offering a buffer against the challenges encountered on the journey to adulthood. Identifying supportive individuals—whether friends, family members, or mentors—is a crucial step in this process. These relationships provide not only a safety net during times of crisis but also an ongoing sense of belonging and community.

Friends often act as our closest confidants, sharing similar experiences and understanding the nuances of daily life. They offer empathy and companionship, which are invaluable when navigating complex emotions or situations. Family members, on the other hand, can provide stability and wisdom gleaned from experience. Their unconditional love often acts as a secure base, helping young adults feel anchored amidst life's uncertainty. Mentors bring yet another layer to this support system by offering guidance and insight into career, educational, or personal challenges, based on their own journeys and expertise.

However, relying solely on one source of support can be limiting. Diversifying sources of support is vital. By including peers, professionals like counselors or therapists, and even online support communities, young adults can ensure they have comprehensive emotional backing tailored to their varied needs. Peers provide relatable insights and shared experiences, whereas professionals offer tools and strategies for handling specific issues more effectively. Online communities might seem unconventional, but they present opportunities to connect with others worldwide who face similar challenges, providing both anonymity and solidarity.

The strength of any support network lies in effective communication. Transparent, open communication fosters trust and strengthens relationships, making it easier to reach out during difficult times. Regular, meaningful conversations with friends and family reinforce bonds and readiness to support each other. When crises arise, established trust facilitates quicker responses and more effective interventions, reducing the impact of stressors.

Moreover, nurturing these support networks is not a one-time effort but requires ongoing commitment. Consistent engagement—through regular meetups, calls, or check-ins—ensures that relationships remain strong and reliable. This continuous investment solidifies the foundation of these networks, ensuring they provide consistent emotional backing whenever needed. In nurturing these relationships, there should be a balance between give and take; supporting others while accepting help when necessary creates a healthy dynamic that fosters resilience in all parties involved.

Building and maintaining such networks does more than just cushion the impact of stress. It contributes significantly to one's overall well-being by promoting positive mental health, enhancing self-esteem, and encouraging personal growth. Being part of a supportive community instills a sense of purpose and belonging, empowering young adults to handle life's uncertainties with greater confidence and poise. Engaging in activities that strengthen these connections—like participating in group events or committing to shared goals—further enhances this sense of community.

Learn to Reframe Negative Thoughts Constructively

Navigating the complexities of adulthood requires young people to cultivate emotional resilience, a key part of which is transforming negative thoughts into constructive perspectives. Understanding and addressing cognitive distortions—such as catastrophizing or overgeneralizing—can significantly influence one's emotional well-being. These distortions are common traps in thinking that lead us down inaccurate paths. Catastrophizing, for instance, involves blowing things out of proportion, assuming the worst will happen, like expecting to fail an exam and, consequently, drop out of school entirely. On the other hand, overgeneralizing takes a single event and turns it into a never-ending pattern. Both distortions negatively impact how we perceive ourselves and the world, creating barriers to happiness and success.

The first step toward overcoming these mental hurdles is recognizing them. This involves increasing your awareness of when and where these distortions occur. For example, if you notice heightened anxiety before tests, identifying this pattern helps you prepare mentally. Awareness acts as a foundation for change, enabling you to catch distorted thoughts before they spiral out of control (Ackerman, 2018).

Once you've identified these patterns, employing a structured method to reframe your thinking can be transformative. Cognitive restructuring is a technique used to shift such detrimental thought patterns into more positive and realistic ones. Begin by questioning the accuracy of your thoughts: Are they based on emotions or facts? What evidence supports or refutes them? For example, if a friend cancels plans, instead of thinking they don't value your friendship, consider more benign reasons, such as their need to handle unexpected commitments. By systematically challenging and replacing distorted thoughts with factual reassessments, emotional regulation improves substantially (Stanborough, 2023).

Alongside this method, positive affirmations serve as valuable tools in altering negative self-beliefs. They work by embedding positive, unconscious changes into daily thought processes. For young adults, who might struggle with self-doubt or imposter syndrome, repeating affirmations like "I am capable and deserving of success" can gradually reshape internal narratives. Historical evidence suggests that consistent practice of affirmations enhances self-worth and confidence, making individuals more resilient to setbacks.

Furthermore, considering alternative perspectives is another crucial strategy. It involves consciously opting to view situations from different angles, which broadens understanding and reduces the perceived significance of negative thoughts. Imagine yourself stuck in traffic, late for an important meeting. Instead of succumbing to frustration, reframe the scenario positively—use the time to plan your meeting agenda or listen to an inspiring podcast. This cognitive flexibility not only alleviates stress but also equips young adults with a skill set essential for adapting to varied life challenges.

Creating a personal coping inventory acts as a practical guideline in this journey. By listing and reviewing personal strategies regularly, young adults can identify effective techniques that aid in reframing thoughts and enhancing cognitive flexibility. This inventory serves as a toolkit for moments of distress, offering different approaches tailored to individual needs. Engaging in self-reflection through techniques like journaling can further support this process. Writing about thoughts and experiences often illuminates underlying patterns and uncovers hidden cognitive distortions. This reflective practice encourages personal growth and offers deeper insights into one's emotional landscape.

Incorporating these methods into one's lifestyle fosters a proactive mindset, encouraging habitual positive thinking. As young adults navigate the demands of academia, work, and relationships, these skills become vital in maintaining balance and fulfilling emotional health. It's about crafting a mental habit loop where identifying distortions, applying reframing techniques, using affirmations, and adopting alternative viewpoints become second nature.

Real-life applications can significantly reinforce the benefits of these strategies. Consider a young professional facing criticism at work; instead of internalizing this feedback negatively, viewing it as an opportunity for growth promotes a healthier perspective. Similarly, college students managing academic pressures benefit from these techniques, as shifting focus from a fixed mindset of failure to a growth mindset of learning transforms their educational experience.

Break Down Overwhelming Tasks into Manageable Steps

Managing overwhelming responsibilities is a crucial aspect of developing emotional resilience, especially for young adults navigating the complexities of adulthood. Overwhelm often arises when responsibilities outpace our capacity to manage them, leading to heightened anxiety and decreased productivity. Recognizing what triggers feelings of being overwhelmed can pave the way for proactive management strategies that prevent stress from escalating.

One effective strategy is breaking tasks into smaller, more manageable steps. This approach provides clarity and direction, transforming daunting projects into achievable goals. Tools like to-do lists are invaluable in this process, as they enable individuals to organize their tasks by priority and progress. By breaking down tasks, focus is enhanced, making it easier to tackle one step at a time. This method not only increases efficiency but also reduces the mental burden of having too much on one's plate at once.

Setting realistic timelines is another significant factor in managing stress. Unrealistic deadlines can create unnecessary pressure, leading to frustration and burnout. When timelines are adjustable, they allow room for unexpected changes, such as personal emergencies or additional work responsibilities. Such flexibility promotes gentle self-management and sustains motivation by accommodating life's unpredictability. It is important to acknowledge that life rarely goes according to plan; therefore, building buffers into timelines can help maintain a steady workflow without succumbing to stress.

Celebrating progress through small victories is key to maintaining motivation. Each accomplishment, no matter how minor, reinforces a positive mindset and encourages continued effort. This practice shifts the focus from what remains undone to what has been achieved, fostering a sense of accomplishment and satisfaction. The act of acknowledging achievements, even if it's just crossing off items on a to-do list, can uplift spirits and instill confidence in one's ability to handle future challenges.

Incorporating time management techniques can further aid in reducing anxiety. For instance, prioritizing tasks using methods like the Eisenhower Matrix can help ensure that the most important duties are completed first, while non-essential ones are either delegated or eliminated. Such an approach allows individuals to focus on what truly matters, alleviating the overload that comes with juggling multiple responsibilities. Techniques like time blocking can also enhance productivity by allocating specific times for focused work, thereby minimizing distractions and improving concentration.

Maintaining organization plays a pivotal role in managing overwhelm. A disorganized workspace can contribute to feelings of stress and chaos. By creating a structured setup, tasks become more visible and approachable. Moreover, an organized environment can prevent missed deadlines and overlooked duties—common sources of work-related anxiety. Implementing methods like the Getting Things Done (GTD) framework can systematize task management, ensuring everything is tracked and easily accessible.

The importance of clear boundaries cannot be overstated. In a culture where work and personal life often blur, setting and adhering to boundaries is essential for preserving mental well-being. Learning to say "no" when at capacity prevents overcommitment and ensures that responsibilities remain manageable. Communicating transparently with peers and superiors about workload and limitations fosters understanding and support within professional environments.

While achieving balance might seem elusive at times, having a strong support system can provide much-needed emotional backing. Engaging with friends, family, or colleagues in open conversations about stressors and duties can offer different perspectives and solutions that may not have been previously considered. These interactions not only relieve stress but also reinforce bonds and provide moral support.

Finally, seeking professional guidance when necessary

should be seen as a productive step rather than a last resort. Experts can offer tailored strategies for coping with overwhelming responsibilities, helping individuals develop personalized plans that suit their unique circumstances.

Establish Boundaries to Protect Your Energy

In navigating the complexities of adulthood, establishing personal boundaries is crucial for maintaining emotional and mental energy. Boundaries serve as protective lines that define your personal space, safeguarding your well-being by regulating interactions with others. By understanding their vital role, you can prevent emotional exhaustion and create a foundation for healthier relationships.

Personal boundaries act as an invisible shield for emotional safety, helping to maintain clarity about your own needs and limits. They define where you end and someone else begins, preventing the seepage of unwanted stressors into your life. This demarcation is essential not only in physical spaces but also emotionally, allowing you to keep your feelings intact and manage stress more effectively. For instance, declining invites to events when you need alone time or choosing not to engage in conversations that drain your energy are ways to protect this space. When these boundaries are clearly set, they help to minimize feelings of overwhelm and undervaluation that can compromise mental health over time (The Importance of Personal Boundaries for Mental Wellness, 2024).

An essential component of healthy boundaries is the ability to communicate them clearly to others. This involves expressing what you find acceptable and what you don't, thereby minimizing misunderstandings. Communication assists others in respecting your limits and sees them as a part of mutual respect. Moreover, it enhances your advocacy skills, enabling you to assertively state your needs without fear of conflict. Imagine a scenario at work where colleagues frequently interrupt your concentration; politely yet firmly stating your need for uninterrupted time cultivates a culture of respect while boosting your productivity.

The art of saying no without feeling guilty is another pivotal aspect of maintaining effective boundaries. Many young adults wrestle with this concept, often equating no with disappointment or rejection. However, recognizing that prioritizing personal needs leads to reduced stress is liberating. Saying no allows you to focus on commitments that matter most to you, facilitating a life of fulfillment rather than resentment. Next time you're asked to take on additional tasks but feel stretched thin, remember that it's okay to decline graciously. By doing so, you honor your own limitations, which ultimately translates into more genuine engagements and less emotional clutter.

Boundaries are not static; regular reassessment ensures they align with your evolving emotional needs. Life is dynamic, and as situations change, so might your requirements for personal space. Engaging in self-reflection helps identify areas where adjustments may be necessary. For example, an introverted college student who initially needed solitary study time might later thrive in group settings due to developed confidence and social skills. Constant evaluation prevents stagnation, fostering self-awareness and encouraging proactive engagement with life changes.

To implement these boundary-setting practices successfully, consider several practical steps. Start by identifying your comfort zones—what feels right and what doesn't. Understanding these limits forms the groundwork for creating clear boundaries. Once established, practice assertive communication using 'I' statements, such as, "I need downtime after work to recharge." This fosters dialogue grounded in mutual respect. Additionally, remain attuned to your feelings; discomfort often signals that boundaries are being pushed, prompting timely reassessment.

It's equally important to cultivate resilience against external pressures that challenge these boundaries. Society and relationships sometimes exert subtle influence to conform, especially in workplace environments. Steadfastness in adhering to your personal values amidst such pressures maintains integrity and balances mental health. Remember, boundaries are as much about what you let in as what you keep out—choose interactions that nourish rather than deplete you.

Integrating and maintaining these boundaries can initially feel daunting, particularly if you've been conditioned to prioritize others' needs. Over time, though, they become second nature, leading to profound shifts in how you experience life and relationships. You'll notice that consistent enforcement of these limits results in more harmonious connections, as ambiguity about roles and expectations fades away.

Regular check-ins with yourself are instrumental in ensuring you're upholding your boundaries, especially during high-stress times or significant life transitions. Consider how your current engagements align with your desired lifestyle and whether they're conducive to your well-being. Self-care practices like journaling or meditation can aid in this reflective process, offering clarity and insight into necessary changes.

Bringing It All Together

Throughout this chapter, we've explored key strategies to help you build emotional resilience when faced with challenges and stress. Recognizing the difference between healthy and unhealthy coping mechanisms is vital. By focusing on positive outlets like exercise, social interaction, and creative pursuits, you can create a solid foundation for your mental well-being. These activities not only lift your mood but also connect you with supportive networks that alleviate feelings of isolation. On the flip side, steering clear from harmful behaviors such as substance abuse or self-criticism prevents deeper emotional issues. Understanding personal boundaries also plays a crucial role in maintaining energy levels and reducing overwhelm, as it helps manage responsibilities effectively.

As you navigate adulthood, remember that developing emotional resilience is a journey requiring patience and commitment. Implement techniques like breaking daunting tasks into smaller steps and reframing negative thoughts constructively. Building a support network around you—friends, family, mentors, or even online communities—ensures you are not alone in this process. Embracing professional guidance when needed can offer tailored solutions specific to your needs. By consistently applying these strategies, you'll not only be better equipped to face life's hurdles but will also lay the groundwork for a balanced and fulfilling future.

6

Cultivating Inner Peace

Finding Tranquility Through Self-Reflection and Mental Decluttering

Finding tranquility through self-reflection and mental decluttering is an insightful journey many young adults undertake while transitioning into adulthood. This pursuit of inner peace often feels like an uphill battle as school, work, and personal relationships pile on simultaneously, making life appear more chaotic than calm. By focusing inward and streamlining what clutters the mind, individuals can unlock profound serenity that might otherwise seem elusive amidst daily stresses. Whether you're a college student grappling with coursework or a young professional navigating corporate expectations, honing the skill of self-reflection to address internal clutter serves as a pivotal tool for achieving balance.

This chapter elegantly unfolds holistic approaches to guide you towards mental clarity by leveraging various lifestyle adjustments. You will discover how organizing your environment can directly impact your mental state, setting the tone for a calmer existence. Additionally, the chapter delves into the concept of taking regular digital detoxes, allowing your mind to unwind from constant online stimulation. You'll explore visualization techniques designed to relax and rejuvenate the spirit through guided imagery exercises. Personal rituals, crafted to ground emotions during life's hectic moments, provide practical ways to manage stress. Finally, understanding mindful media consumption enlightens readers about maintaining a healthy mental state in today's fast-paced world. With these insights, young adults, students, and professionals alike can carve out peaceful sanctuaries within their minds, nurturing a stable foundation upon which to build fulfilling lives.

Organize Your Living Space to Reduce Chaos

Imagine waking up to a room filled with clutter—piles of clothes on the floor, papers strewn across your desk, and random items crowding every open space. Such a setting can be overwhelming and produce an internal disarray that disrupts mental clarity. Contrastingly, stepping into a well-organized environment can immediately evoke a sense of calm and focus. This difference isn't merely cosmetic; it's deeply psychological.

A cluttered space often mirrors a cluttered mind. When our surroundings are chaotic, it becomes challenging to concentrate or feel at peace. The visual distraction from untidy spaces can lead to increased stress levels and a feeling of being perpetually behind. Psychologically, clutter can drain cognitive resources, making it harder to process information and manage emotions effectively. Studies have shown that women who describe their homes as messy have elevated levels of cortisol, the stress hormone, compared to those who consider their living spaces orderly (*Mental Health Benefits of Decluttering*, 2021).

Creating a tidy environment might seem daunting, but employing specific decluttering strategies can transform this task into a manageable and even enjoyable process. A popular method is the 'one in, one out' rule, which involves donating or disposing of an item whenever a new one is acquired. This not only maintains balance but also encourages thoughtful consumption. Starting small is another practical approach. Tackling just one drawer or shelf at a time prevents overwhelm and provides a series of quick wins that encourage continued effort. Structuring regular decluttering sessions into your schedule can gradually lead to a more organized home, fostering an atmosphere ripe for relaxation and reduced stress.

Adding elements of nature to your space can amplify these benefits. Introducing indoor plants contributes to a calming ambiance, as greenery has been linked to reducing anxiety and promoting deeper breathing. Soft lighting, such as dimmable lamps or candles, can create an inviting warmth that encourages mindfulness. Together, these enhancements support a soothing environment that helps ground you mentally and emotionally after hectic days.

Beyond the initial act of organizing, turning tidiness into a daily habit can yield long-lasting positive effects. Incorporating simple routines, like tidying before bed or spending ten minutes each day arranging one space, can embed organization into the fabric of your lifestyle. These habits can eventually become second nature, requiring minimal effort while continuously offering serenity and order. Over time, these minor adjustments accumulate to significantly alter your mental landscape, leading to improved mood, enhanced productivity, and greater overall life satisfaction.

For young adults facing the uncertainties of early adulthood—be it through school, work, or personal relationships—a structured living space can serve as an anchor. It's a controllable element in an ever-changing world. College students especially can benefit from having a clean, organized study area to boost concentration and efficiency amid academic pressures. Similarly, young professionals looking to establish routines for success will find that starting with a decluttered workspace sets a productive tone.

Engage in Weekly Digital Detoxes

Living in our hyper-connected world, we've become accustomed to the constant pinging of notifications, emails demanding immediate attention, and social media vying for our focus. While these digital interactions are an integral part of modern life, they can cumulatively lead to digital overload, causing anxiety and mental exhaustion. It's essential to recognize this pattern and actively seek moments of tranquility by unplugging from technology.

Continuous connectivity can overwhelm us, leaving little room for genuine reflection or personal peace. The barrage of information and interaction often feels like a never-ending treadmill, where stepping off seems challenging but is crucial for mental health. This nonstop digital engagement leads not only to increased stress levels but also impacts our ability to focus and be present in our real-life interactions. Anxiety stemming from constant connectivity is common among young adults navigating school, work, and social lives. By understanding that much of this stress originates from digital sources, we can start to address it effectively.

One effective approach to mitigating this stress involves planning dedicated screen-free times. Scheduling these breaks intentionally allows the mind to recharge and offers a profound sense of relief. Imagine setting aside a few hours during your weekend when you put all devices away, perhaps during a leisurely breakfast or a walk in the park. These device-free periods act as a sanctuary from digital chaos, offering breathing space for our thoughts and enabling us to engage with the world around us more meaningfully.

Similarly, setting usage boundaries helps carve out time for activities that don't involve screens, promoting relaxation and mindfulness. Consider instituting tech-free zones within your living space—places where gadgets are off-limits, like the dining area or bedroom. These zones allow for quality interactions with family or roommates without the distraction of screens, fostering deeper connections. Engaging in activities away from devices—such as reading a book, meditating, or exercising—not only refreshes the mind but imbues a sense of balance into our daily routines.

Periodically disconnecting from technology is not just about breaking away from screens; it's an invitation to reconnect with oneself and the environment. These pauses contribute significantly to improving mood and sleep quality. The blue light emitted by screens can interfere with the natural sleeping patterns, making it harder to fall asleep and enjoy restful nights. Creating a habit of turning off devices an hour before bedtime encourages a healthier sleep cycle, which enhances overall mood and productivity the following day.

Moreover, these periods of disconnection provide time for reflection and self-discovery. In the quietude, devoid of digital interruptions, we have the opportunity to ponder over our aspirations, evaluate our mental well-being, and recognize the simple joys of everyday life—like watching a sunrise or sharing a moment with friends. Reconnecting with nature or indulging in creative pursuits nurtures inner peace, helping restore balance between our digital and analogue worlds.

While stepping away from technology offers tangible benefits, maintaining this balance requires thoughtful reintegration of technology post-detox. Establishing guidelines ensures that the return to digital life is both mindful and measured. One strategy involves being selective about the apps and notifications you allow on your devices. Prioritize those that add value or necessity while limiting ones that frequently disrupt focus or peace. Techniques such as setting specific times for checking email or social media can curb excessive use and foster healthier habits.

Equally important, cultivate digital practices that support personal growth rather than detract from it. For instance, using technology to learn new skills or participate in enriching online communities can be empowering. Harnessing the vast resources available digitally for educational and cultural enrichment can turn screen time into a constructive activity rather than a mindless escape.

Building self-awareness about one's digital habits and seeking balance leads to enhanced mental clarity and resilience. Young adults, college students, and professionals alike will find that intentional unplugging empowers them to tackle life's challenges with greater composure and creativity. Embracing these practices promotes not just momentary relief, but lasting transformation in how we interact with the digital realm, leading to a more fulfilling and less stressful lifestyle.

Practice Guided Imagery for Relaxation

Imagine closing your eyes and finding yourself on a tranquil beach, with soft waves gently lapping the shore. This simple act of visualization, known as guided imagery, is a powerful tool for relaxation and cultivating inner peace. By immersing yourself in calming mental scenarios, like being in a serene forest or sitting by a peaceful lake, you can rejuvenate your spirit and find respite from the chaotic pace of everyday life. Guided imagery serves as a bridge to tranquility, allowing your mind to rest even when your body cannot.

The effectiveness of these visualizations can be magnified by engaging your senses and incorporating deep breathing. For instance, while picturing yourself in a meadow, take a moment to smell the blooming flowers, feel the warmth of the sun on your skin, and listen to the chirping birds. Coupling these sensory details with slow, deep breaths not only brings the imagined scenario to life but also helps to calm your nervous system. Deep breathing serves as an anchor, grounding you in the present moment and enhancing the overall experience.

It allows your body to switch from a state of tension to one of relaxation, opening up space for peace to permeate your being.

Personalization of these images adds another layer of richness to the practice. Imagine wandering through your favorite park, hearing the rustling leaves and feeling the cool breeze— your mind knows this place, and it's where you feel at ease. Revisiting familiar locations or happy memories makes the visualizations more relatable and effective for stress relief. When you design these scenes, you ensure they resonate deeply with your personal experiences, allowing for a more profound sense of calmness and comfort. Through visualization, we remind ourselves of spaces and moments that bring us joy, reinforcing positive emotions and relieving stress.

Incorporating guided imagery into daily life offers significant benefits, especially during times of stress or right before sleep. Think of it as a mini-retreat that fits into your schedule whenever needed. During the hectic moments of a busy day, pausing for even a few minutes to escape mentally can shift your perspective and lighten your mood. Visualization becomes a tool you carry with you, one that is always accessible when you need to reset and recharge your mindset. Regular practice of these techniques fosters a positive outlook, as your mind learns to seek out and create soothing environments amidst chaos.

When bedtime approaches, using guided imagery can become part of your nighttime ritual. Visualizing peaceful settings can induce relaxation, making it easier to drift into restful sleep, which is crucial for maintaining mental health and clarity. The reduction in anxiety and improved sleep quality observed in studies underscores the power of visualization as an ally against the pressures of modern life (West, 2022). By committing just a small portion of your evening to mental imagery, you set the stage for a restorative night's rest.

To make these benefits a staple in your routine, consider approaching guided imagery with deliberate intention. Start by setting aside a regular time each day—whether it's during a lunch break, after work, or as part of your evening wind-down. Choose a quiet space where interruptions are minimal, turning off devices to maintain focus. Begin each session with a few deep breaths to relax your body and mind, then let your imagination take the lead.

Creating a personalized visualization might initially require some experimentation. You might find inspiration from audio guides available in apps or online, or prefer crafting your ideal scene from scratch. Some people benefit from imagining themselves achieving goals, like acing an exam or excelling at work, as these scenarios can boost confidence and reduce performance-related anxiety. Others may focus on natural landscapes or cherished memories. Customize this practice until it reflects what brings you comfort and joy, ensuring it aligns with your unique preferences and needs.

By integrating guided imagery consistently into your life, you not only build a refuge from stress but also cultivate a habit of positivity. This proactive approach to mental well-being is particularly relevant for young adults navigating the complexities of adulthood. As college students juggle academic pressures alongside social commitments, and young professionals face workplace demands, guided imagery offers a straightforward method to manage emotions and enhance overall mental health.

Develop a Grounding Ritual to Use When Stressed

Establishing a grounding ritual can be incredibly beneficial in navigating the chaos and stress of everyday life. Grounding practices serve as a powerful tool to bring us into the present moment, offering a sense of control and tranquility when everything feels overwhelming. Picture this: you're standing in the middle of a storm, wind whipping around you, but you have an anchor, a steady force that keeps you upright and calm. That's what grounding exercises aim to achieve.

These techniques act as a bridge between our often scattered thoughts and the stability of the present moment. By focusing on something tangible or specific—like our breath or the feeling of grass underfoot—it's possible to break the cycle of anxiety. This reestablishment of control is crucial for maintaining mental clarity and emotional resilience. When you hit those inevitable rough patches, grounding can be your internal chill pill, helping you face challenges with a steadier mindset.

Simple grounding methods are key, and it's essential to choose ones that resonate personally because there's no one-size-fits-all approach. Breathing exercises are among the most accessible. Try the technique where you count to four as you inhale, hold for seven, and exhale for eight. It's a method lauded for its capacity to soothe the nervous system and return focus back to the now. Sensory focus can also play a pivotal role. Imagine holding a small stone and concentrating on its texture and weight, feeling it ground you through touch alone.

Finding the right practice requires experimentation. You might discover that sitting quietly and visualizing roots growing from your feet gives you stability while another person finds solace in movement, like shaking off tension through ecstatic dance. The journey to finding your effective personal ritual can be enlightening. Allow yourself the freedom to explore different practices, paying attention to how each makes you feel, and which ones truly alleviate your anxiety. Your body and mind will naturally gravitate towards certain exercises; listen and make note of these preferences.

Guidelines for establishing these personal rituals suggest starting small and integrating them into daily life. Consistency is the secret ingredient here. You might begin or end your day with a few minutes of focused breathing, gradually weaving it into your routine until it becomes second nature. Intentionally place your grounding moments throughout your day—while commuting, during breaks at work, or before sleep. These intentional pauses not only help maintain peace but also build emotional resilience over time.

Developing a customized ritual means embracing trial and error. Ask yourself questions like, "What makes me feel secure?" or "When do I feel most at ease during my day?" Use these insights to shape your unique ritual. Journaling can be helpful in recording your experiences with different practices, enabling you to track what works best and adjust as needed.

Moreover, don't underestimate the value of layering multiple techniques. Combining approaches, such as mindful breathing with visualization or gentle yoga stretches, can deepen the impact, providing a multi-sensory experience that reinforces your connection to the present.

Incorporating grounding into daily routines promotes long-term mental health benefits. It creates a buffer against life's stressors by enhancing your ability to remain calm and centered amid chaos. As these practices become habit, they form a protective shield, reducing the likelihood of being swept away by anxiety.

As young adults and professionals, the demands of school, work, and relationships can often pull you in every direction. Establishing a grounding ritual will equip you with a reliable toolkit to manage these pressures effectively. It's about taking proactive steps to prioritize self-care and emotional well-being amidst all the demands.

Limit Exposure to Distressing News

In today's fast-paced world, the constant barrage of news and media can have a profound effect on our mental well-being. While staying informed is important, overexposure to negative media can lead to increased anxiety and a numbing of our emotional responses. The psychological impact of continuously engaging with distressing headlines, sensationalized stories, or emotionally charged content cannot be underestimated. Many young adults find themselves caught in a cycle where they feel obligated to keep up with the latest news, often at the expense of their mental peace.

Research has shown that continuous exposure to negative news can amplify feelings of stress and anxiety. This often results in a state of desensitization, where individuals become less responsive to real-life events, feeling overwhelmed and unable to process emotions properly. The relentless flow of disturbing information can create a skewed perception of reality, leading to heightened vigilance and worry, which is detrimental to one's overall well-being.

Establishing boundaries around news consumption is crucial in mitigating these negative impacts. By scheduling specific times for catching up on news, individuals can limit their exposure, thus reducing the adverse effects on mental health. This deliberate approach allows people to remain informed without becoming overwhelmed. For instance, dedicating 15-30 minutes a day to watching or reading the news, preferably from sources known for balanced reporting, can help maintain a healthy mental space while still being engaged with worldly events. Setting such boundaries empowers individuals to take control over the type of information they consume and its timing, ultimately fostering a more peaceful state of mind.

In addition to setting boundaries, exploring alternative media sources that prioritize positivity and constructive narratives can be highly beneficial. Consuming content that highlights uplifting stories, innovative solutions, or progress in various fields counters the negativity bias prevalent in mainstream news. Alternative media platforms that focus on community successes, scientific breakthroughs, or human interest stories provide a sense of hope and inspiration. These positive inputs nourish the mind and contribute to a more balanced perspective on life, promoting mental resilience.

Moreover, actively seeking involvement in local initiatives can significantly enhance well-being by providing a sense of agency and fostering community connections. Participation in community projects or volunteering offers a dual benefit: it detaches individuals from the virtual realm of negative media and engages them in tangible, productive activities. This active engagement instills a sense of purpose and belonging, reinforcing the realization that one can indeed make a difference, however small, in their environment.

By becoming part of local environmental clean-ups, educational programs, or social causes, individuals not only contribute positively to society but also build lasting relationships within their communities. These connections serve as a support system, offering emotional sustenance far beyond what digital interactions can provide. The act of collaborating with others towards a shared goal strengthens interpersonal bonds and enriches one's social network, which is vital for emotional health.

Young professionals and college students, particularly those navigating the demands of academia and early career challenges, can greatly benefit from these strategies. Limiting exposure to stressful media while engaging in positive, community-centered activities provides a practical framework for managing stress effectively. As this demographic seeks ways to balance academic pressures and personal growth, incorporating mindful media consumption practices becomes essential.

Incorporating these approaches into daily life does not require drastic lifestyle changes. Simple adjustments like choosing specific time slots to check the news, subscribing to newsletters that share positive stories, or joining local hobby groups will gradually transform one's media interaction habits. Over time, these changes can cultivate a healthier relationship with media, enhancing mental clarity and emotional stability.

Final Thoughts

As we've explored throughout this chapter, achieving mental clarity and peace is not a one-step process but a holistic journey. We've delved into various strategies, beginning with the impact of organizing your living space to reduce chaos. A tidy environment isn't just about order; it reflects and enhances our mental state. By adopting methods like decluttering and incorporating nature into our surroundings, we create spaces that encourage calmness and focus. This chapter also highlighted the benefits of digital detoxification as an essential tool for fighting stress in our hyper-connected world. Establishing regular screen-free times allows us to recharge and find tranquility away from digital distractions. Whether through setting tech-free zones or engaging in activities without screens, these habits promote better mental health and enhance our real-life interactions.

We've also learned that practices such as guided imagery and grounding rituals offer powerful ways to manage stress and cultivate inner peace. Visualization techniques allow us to retreat mentally to serene places, providing respites from life's chaos. Similarly, grounding exercises bring us back to the present moment, offering stability during turbulent times. Developing personal rituals that resonate with us can become invaluable anchors amidst life's demands. Lastly, we've touched on mindful media consumption, which involves setting boundaries and seeking positive narratives to maintain emotional resilience. By integrating these holistic approaches, young adults, students, and professionals alike can build balanced routines that foster mental clarity and overall well-being as they navigate life's various challenges.

7

Defining Your Life Purpose

Uncovering Your Purpose and Aligning Life's Direction

Discovering your purpose and aligning it with the direction of your life can be one of the most rewarding journeys you embark on. Think about those moments when everything seems to click, when your actions reflect who you are at your core. This sense of alignment often brings a profound sense of fulfillment and happiness. But for many people, especially young adults stepping into the world of adult responsibilities, finding this harmony can be challenging. The pressures of school, work, and relationships often overshadow personal aspirations, making it difficult to pinpoint and pursue what truly matters. Yet, within this hectic landscape lies an opportunity to pause, reflect, and realign with what makes life genuinely meaningful.

In this chapter, we delve into practical strategies to help you uncover and clarify your purpose. It's not just about identifying what is important to you but also about aligning those values with your daily life. We explore how differentiating between your personal beliefs and societal expectations can lead to a more authentic existence. You'll find techniques to help integrate these values into everyday actions, thus turning abstract concepts into tangible parts of your life. Additionally, you'll learn about visualization methods that allow you to imagine your desired future and work backward to make it a reality. Setting both short-term and long-term goals aligned with your passions will be a key focus, providing you with actionable steps toward building a life that resonates with your inner values. Through reflection and adaptation, you'll discover how to maintain flexibility in your pursuits, ensuring personal growth and fulfillment as your journey evolves. With this guidance, you're invited to chart a course that celebrates your unique strengths and aspirations, creating a life that feels true to you.

Identify Your Core Values and Beliefs

Clarifying what truly matters to you is a vital step on the journey toward living an authentic and fulfilling life. It involves distinguishing between personal values and societal expectations, reflecting on how beliefs shape decisions, and using practical exercises to articulate one's core values. By integrating these values into daily actions, individuals can enhance their overall satisfaction and sense of purpose.

Understanding the difference between personal values and societal expectations is crucial in promoting authentic living. Often, people find themselves conforming to external pressures and norms without questioning if these align with their genuine beliefs and desires. For example, many young adults may feel pushed towards certain career paths or lifestyles that are traditionally seen as successful. However, it's important to pause and question whether these choices resonate with their personal aspirations and values. The Peter Thiel Question, "What important truth do very few people agree with you on?" can be useful here, encouraging self-reflection to uncover beliefs that aren't simply inherited or absorbed from others (7 Ways to Discover and Clarify Your Personal Values, 2020).

Reflecting on how our beliefs influence our decisions and capacity for change is another key aspect. Our actions are often guided by deeply held convictions, which may go unexamined for long periods. By regularly assessing these beliefs, we can understand their origins—be it family influence, cultural norms, or personal experiences—and determine whether they continue to serve us well. This process allows us to challenge outdated beliefs, embrace new perspectives, and foster change when necessary. Such reflection not only aids in personal growth but also supports making intentional decisions that align with who we truly are at our core.

Engaging in exercises like journaling and discussions can help clarify and articulate your core values. Journaling offers a private space to explore thoughts and emotions, providing insights into what genuinely matters. Questions such as, "What brings me joy?" or "When do I feel most alive?" can spark deeper understanding. Similarly, conversations with trusted friends or mentors can provide fresh viewpoints, helping to refine and solidify your values. It's through these reflective practices that you might realize, for instance, that the pursuit of creative expression holds more significance than a high-paying job, leading to lifestyle changes that better align with this newly acknowledged value.

Incorporating clarified values into daily actions enhances life satisfaction. Once you identify what truly matters, the next step is weaving those values into your everyday routine. If health and well-being are high on your list, consider setting aside time each day for physical activity, meditation, or preparing nutritious meals. Aligning actions with values transforms abstract concepts into tangible parts of your life, resulting in greater fulfillment and coherence between your inner world and outer actions.

It's worth noting that this alignment requires conscious effort and sometimes courage. There may be moments when choosing to act according to your values conflicts with societal expectations or leads to difficult choices. For example, valuing familial relationships might mean moving closer to home despite having promising career opportunities elsewhere. While challenging, maintaining consistency between values and actions ultimately fosters a stronger sense of integrity and contentment.

To guide this integration effectively, one could create a personal vision statement. This statement serves as a manifesto capturing the person you aspire to be, the qualities you wish to cultivate, and the habits you intend to build. An ideal personal vision statement should reflect your values and provide clarity on the kind of life you envision for yourself. It acts as a beacon during decision-making processes, reminding you of your true north whenever confronted with choices that test your commitment to your values.

Visualize Your Ideal Future and Work Backward

Defining your life's purpose is a journey that can be greatly aided by visualization. Imagine this: You wake up each day with clarity, knowing exactly what you're striving for and why. Visualization helps you to craft a vivid vision of your ideal life, which significantly boosts motivation. When you see yourself succeeding in various aspects of your life, from career achievements to personal growth, it creates a mental image that fuels your drive to make those visions a reality.

Crafting a vision begins with identifying what truly matters to you. Envision your perfect day—from the moment you wake up, consider how you feel, who you're surrounded by, and what activities fill your hours. Visualize where you live, the kind of work you do, and importantly, how all these elements make you feel fulfilled and purposeful. By exploring these details, you create a vibrant blueprint of your desired life, which serves as a motivational anchor.

Once you have a clear vision, the next step is breaking down the steps needed to achieve it, transforming your dreams into an actionable roadmap. Begin by setting concrete milestones— these are smaller, achievable goals that lead to your ultimate vision. For instance, if your goal is to start a business, initial milestones might include researching your industry, drafting a business plan, or securing funding. Each milestone reached acts as a stepping stone, providing motivation and tangible progress toward your larger goals.

A powerful tool often recommended in this process is a vision board. Vision boards serve as daily inspiration and a creative outlet, reinforcing your aspirations through visual means. This board could be a collage of pictures, quotes, and symbols that resonate with your dreams. The idea is to place your vision board somewhere you'll see it frequently—a constant reminder of what you're working towards. Engaging in this creative process not only cements your commitment but also invites collaboration; creating vision boards with friends or peers can foster collective creativity and support. Citing Perry (2023), vision boards can be a conduit for manifesting your dream life by keeping your goals at the forefront of your mind and encouraging intentional action.

Aligning daily actions with your overarching vision ensures consistent progress. Take a moment each day to consider whether your choices and activities align with your mission. Small, deliberate actions can gradually accumulate, bringing your vision closer to reality. This alignment doesn't mean every day will be perfectly productive, but maintaining a focus on your broader purpose helps guide decisions and sustains momentum even when challenges arise.

Moreover, remember that life is dynamic, and your vision can evolve over time. As you grow and circumstances change, regularly revisit and adjust your vision. Update your vision board with new images and ideas that reflect your current aspirations. This practice allows your vision to remain relevant and meaningful, adapting to your personal development and shifting priorities. According to the Journal of Research in Personality, engaging with your evolving vision regularly fosters positivity and enhances the belief that your dreams are within reach (Perry, 2023).

Incorporating these practices into your life isn't just about achieving external success—it's also about internal fulfillment. A strong sense of purpose derived from a clear vision enhances emotional well-being and resilience. It helps balance the rush of modern life, offering a touchstone of meaning amidst stress and challenges. By defining your life's purpose through visualization, you take control of your narrative, directing it toward what genuinely fulfills and excites you.

Visualization is more than an abstract exercise; it's a proactive approach to life planning. As you journey through different stages, from college to young adulthood and into professional life, this technique empowers you to navigate transitions smoothly and intentionally. For young adults grappling with the multitude of changes that life throws their way, the clarity gained from visualization can be a guiding light.

Using visualization techniques offers practical benefits as well. It helps improve focus, encourages strategic thinking, and engenders a positive outlook. When you consistently picture success and happiness, you cultivate an environment conducive to growth and achievement.

Keep in mind that the power of visualization lies in repetition and belief. Regularly picturing your vision and affirming its possibility strengthens your resolve. It's not just about seeing but believing in the reality of your vision. With dedication and persistence, the seemingly distant dreams become reachable goals.

Set Short-Term and Long-Term Goals Aligned with Your Passions

Bridging the gap between aspirations and reality is an essential step in uncovering your purpose and aligning life's direction. Goal-setting serves as a powerful tool in this process, laying a foundation for transforming dreams into achievable targets. Young adults, college students, and young professionals can benefit immensely from structured goal-setting, especially when entering adulthood's complex landscape. Implementing SMART goals is a practical method to enhance clarity and focus, providing a roadmap for success.

SMART goals are Specific, Measurable, Attainable, Realistic, and Time-Limited. This framework guides you in creating well-defined objectives that offer clear direction. Begin by pinpointing specific targets instead of vague aspirations, such as "I want to be fit" versus "I will run three times a week." Break down your goals into measurable components to track progress effectively. For instance, quantify your target by setting milestones like running five kilometers by month-end. You'll need to ensure these milestones are attainable within your current lifestyle constraints, making room for realistic expectations. Finally, incorporate time limitations to create urgency and drive action, like planning to complete your fitness target within three months.

Setting goals aligned with your passions significantly boosts motivation and engagement. When passionate about your pursuits, the journey becomes enjoyable, and commitment happens organically. Imagine you're a young professional interested in photography—integrating this passion into your career aspirations makes your job feel less like work and more like a fulfilling venture. Aligning your goals with something that genuinely excites you fosters resilience, even when challenges arise. It transforms your aspiration into a lifelong pursuit rather than a mere task.

Emphasizing short-term benchmarks is crucial for building confidence and adjusting strategies as needed. Short-term achievements act as stepping stones leading to larger objectives, offering tangible proof of progress. They provide opportunities to reassess your approach, allowing flexibility in tailoring goals to better suit your evolving circumstances. Consider a college student aiming to graduate with honors; setting short-term academic targets, like maintaining a certain GPA each semester, ensures that they remain motivated throughout their studies. These benchmarks don't only celebrate mini-successes but also highlight areas needing improvement, prompting necessary adjustments to achieve long-term success.

Long-term goals, however, require adaptability to life's inevitable changes and evolving visions. As you grow, your priorities might shift, necessitating a reevaluation of what you strive to achieve. This adaptability prevents stagnation and keeps your life's direction aligned with burgeoning insights and experiences. For example, you might start your working life aiming to climb the corporate ladder but later discover an entrepreneurial spirit within you. Adapting your long-term goals to accommodate new interests while still respecting your foundational values is key. Regularly revisiting and revising goals allows you to manage life's unpredictability without losing sight of your purpose.

To fully integrate goal-setting into your life, it's beneficial to engage in exercises that clarify personal values. Values act as a compass, ensuring that goals align with what's truly important to you. Participate in activities like journaling about peak experiences, which can reveal profound insights into your core values. Discussions with mentors or peers enrich understanding, offering diverse perspectives on what could shape your life's path. Utilizing tools like value cards simplifies prioritization, enabling you to focus on essential aspects that matter most.

These practices encourage intentional living—a deliberate choice to pursue goals that resonate deeply with personal convictions. When aligning your life's direction with these identified values, every step taken feels purposeful and fulfilling. You're not just setting random goals; you're crafting a meaningful life story driven by clarity and passion. Whether you aim for academic excellence, professional achievement, or personal growth, firmly anchoring your goals to well-understood values ensures enduring satisfaction and fulfillment.

Challenge Yourself to Step Out of Your Comfort Zone

In the journey of discovering our strengths and potential, challenges play an essential role. They push us beyond the boundaries of our comfort zones, areas where we feel safe and secure but may also become stagnant. By identifying these comfort zones, we can pinpoint growth opportunities that lie just outside them. Just like a plant that has to break through the soil to reach sunlight, real growth often requires breaking through familiar barriers.

Recognizing our comfort zones begins with honest self-reflection. Consider the routines and habits that keep you feeling secure. These could be specific tasks at work that you excel in or social situations you find effortlessly manageable. While comfort isn't inherently detrimental, remaining within its borders for too long can lead to missed opportunities for personal development. To identify areas ripe for growth, ask yourself what activities make you feel uncomfortable or hesitant. These are often indications of where you have the most to learn and grow.

Once you've identified potential areas for growth, the next step is to incrementally face these challenges. It's important not to overwhelm yourself by diving head-first into anxiety-inducing situations. Instead, gradually expose yourself to new experiences or increased responsibilities. This approach builds resilience and reduces fear over time, much like how muscles grow stronger with regular exercise. For instance, if public speaking incites anxiety, start small by speaking up in meetings or joining a discussion group before tackling larger audiences.

By taking these steps, you'll begin to see that discomfort doesn't have to be a negative experience. Embracing discomfort involves staying present in uncomfortable situations and reframing them as opportunities rather than threats. Mindfulness practices can help you remain grounded in the present moment, allowing you to respond thoughtfully rather than react fearfully. Reframing challenges involves viewing them as valuable lessons rather than insurmountable obstacles. Each challenge provides insights that can refine your skills and boost your confidence.

Reflecting on your experiences is crucial for recognizing progress and understanding your evolution. After facing a challenge, take time to assess what you learned and how you've changed. Documenting these reflections can be invaluable, serving as a tangible reminder of your growth journey. Writing down your thoughts allows you to track patterns, understand what strategies worked best, and plan future endeavors. You might realize that what once seemed impossible now feels achievable, indicating significant personal development.

Consider learning from people who have successfully embraced discomfort. Reading about their journeys can provide inspiration and practical insights, highlighting different strategies and outcomes. Seeking feedback from trusted mentors or coaches can also offer guidance and perspective, helping you refine your approach to challenges. Remember that balancing discomfort with self-care is vital. It's important to engage in activities that promote relaxation and recovery, such as meditation or spending time in nature. Listening to your body allows you to maintain your well-being while pursuing growth.

Embrace failure as part of the process. Failure is a natural component of any learning curve, providing opportunities to build resilience. Rather than seeing setbacks as defeat, view them as chances to recalibrate and try again with newfound insight. Every misstep teaches something valuable, potentially leading to greater successes down the road. Adopting a positive outlook on failure can transform your approach to challenges, making them less intimidating and more empowering.

Staying committed to growth while maintaining flexibility is key. Commitment drives perseverance, but being open to changing tactics ensures you're not stuck in approaches that aren't effective. If a strategy isn't yielding results, be willing to explore alternatives. As you grow and learn, your goals may evolve, requiring periodic reassessment to ensure they still align with your values and aspirations.

Reflect Regularly on Your Progress and Adjust Accordingly

Reflection is a powerful tool that can guide us toward a more purposeful life. By taking the time to look inward, we gain insights into our desires, strengths, and the path that aligns best with our values. To effectively utilize reflection in aligning with life purposes, it's crucial to establish structured routines that promote consistent introspection.

Establishing structured routines for reflection means dedicating specific time blocks within your schedule for thoughtful self-examination. Whether it's daily, weekly, or monthly, creating this habit helps ensure that you're regularly assessing where you are versus where you want to be. For many young adults and college students, mornings work well, offering a quiet moment before the day begins. Others might find peace in evening reflections, using the day's experiences as material for thought. These routines don't have to be long; even ten minutes of focused reflection can be incredibly effective. The key is consistency, which, over time, embeds reflection as a natural part of your life rhythm.

When engaging in this regular reflection, it's vital to evaluate both your growth and any setbacks encountered. This balanced approach fosters resilience, an essential skill when navigating life's challenges. By acknowledging achievements, you're able to celebrate progress and reinforce positive behaviors. But examining setbacks is equally important. Instead of viewing these as failures, they can be reframed as learning opportunities. This process not only strengthens your ability to bounce back but also cultivates a mindset that sees obstacles as integral to personal development.

To further enhance this reflective practice, allow flexibility in your goals. Life is unpredictable, and rigidly clinging to initial plans can sometimes lead to frustration or missed opportunities. Flexibility doesn't mean abandoning your objectives; rather, it involves adapting them as circumstances change. For instance, career aspirations might shift after gaining new perspectives through education or travel. Similarly, interpersonal relationships may evolve, leading to different priorities. By remaining open to modifying goals, you create a dynamic alignment with your life purpose that accommodates growth and discovery.

Sharing reflections with peers can provide invaluable support and feedback. Engaging in conversations about your thoughts and experiences offers fresh perspectives and reinforces accountability. Peers who share similar aspirations or challenges can offer advice, encouragement, or simply a listening ear. Whether through informal chats, organized discussion groups, or online communities, these exchanges foster a sense of connection and understanding. Additionally, articulating your reflections often leads to clearer insights, helping solidify your understanding of what truly matters.

Consider starting a reflective journal to track your journey over time. Writing allows you to document thoughts and see how they've evolved, serving as a tangible record of your progress. Include entries on moments of triumph, lessons from setbacks, and evolving insights into your purpose. As you revisit past entries, patterns might emerge, highlighting areas of persistent interest or recurring challenges that need attention. This ongoing narrative becomes a personal guidebook, uniquely tailored to your experience.

Moreover, incorporating mindfulness practices can deepen your reflective efforts. Techniques such as meditation, breathwork, or mindful walking encourage present-moment aware-ness. This focus helps quiet external distractions, enabling a more profound connection with your inner self. These practices don't have to be extensive; even brief sessions can significantly enhance clarity and concentration during reflection.

Finally, remember that reflection is not about reaching immediate conclusions. It's an ongoing process of discovery and realignment. Give yourself permission to explore diverse interests and ideas, knowing that each step brings you closer to uncovering your unique life purpose. Embrace this journey with patience and curiosity, allowing space for unexpected revelations along the way.

Bringing It All Together

As you journey through the process of identifying your pur-pose, aligning values, and setting goals for a rewarding life, remember that these steps are deeply personal and uniquely yours. This chapter has offered practical methods to help you clarify what truly matters, reflect on your beliefs, and connect them to your daily actions. Embracing journaling, open discussions, and vision boards as tools can foster not only self-awareness but also bring clarity to your aspirations. The aim is to transform abstract ideas into tangible parts of your reality, ensuring that your life aligns with who you wish to become.

Taking active measures to visualize your ideal future and break it down into achievable goals emphasizes the importance of living intentionally and authentically. By setting short-term and long-term objectives aligned with your passions, you create a structured yet flexible path forward. As you engage in this ongoing journey, be willing to step out of your comfort zone and embrace both successes and setbacks as opportunities for growth. Regular reflection and adaptation ensure that your strategies remain relevant, resonating with your evolving desires and goals. Remember, this journey isn't just about finding external success—it's about nurturing internal fulfillment and creating a meaningful narrative for yourself.

8

Energizing Your Day

Boost Your Energy Levels with Practical Lifestyle Changes

Boosting your energy levels is all about making practical lifestyle changes that fit seamlessly into your daily routine. Imagine waking up each morning feeling refreshed and ready to take on the world, with a wellspring of energy that lasts throughout your day. That's the kind of vitality we all aspire to achieve, but it often seems elusive amid the hustle and bustle of modern life. The constant juggling act between professional responsibilities, academic pursuits, and social commitments can leave you drained, searching for that extra boost to get through the day. Fortunately, there are simple yet effective strategies that can help you reclaim your energy and maintain it. It starts with understanding how everyday choices—from what you eat to how you move—can significantly impact your energy levels. By making small tweaks in your lifestyle, you can pave the way to a more vibrant and energetic version of yourself.

In this chapter, you'll explore practical strategies designed to enhance your energy naturally. We'll delve into the role of nutrition and discover how making the right dietary choices can fuel your body efficiently. You'll learn how establishing healthier sleep patterns can lead to more restorative rest, leaving you refreshed and vigorous each morning. Movement also plays a crucial role, so we'll look at how incorporating stretches and regular breaks can stave off fatigue during long hours at work or study. Hydration is another key player in keeping your mind sharp and your body functioning optimally, so we'll discuss how maintaining proper fluid intake can be a game-changer. Finally, we'll identify activities that invigorate rather than exhaust, helping you find joy in your daily routine. By the end of this chapter, you'll have a toolkit of ideas to help sustain energy levels, ensuring you're always at your best.

Understand the Balance Between Nutrition and Energy

When it comes to boosting energy levels, one of the most vital elements is nutrition. The connection between what you eat and how energetic you feel is significant. To enhance your vitality, understanding this link can make a considerable difference in your daily life.

Nutrient-dense foods, such as whole grains, fruits, and vegetables, are powerhouse ingredients that can very effectively improve energy levels. These foods are rich sources of essential vitamins and minerals needed for various bodily functions, including energy production. For instance, whole grains like oats, brown rice, and wheat provide complex carbohydrates that break down slowly and ensure a steady release of energy over time. They don't just satisfy hunger but sustain you throughout the day without the spikes and crashes that come from refined carbohydrates.

Fruits and vegetables are not only delicious but also packed with nutrients. Leafy greens, berries, and bananas offer an abundance of vitamins C and A, potassium, and other crucial nutrients. These contribute to proper cell function and immune support, among other roles, which are critical for maintaining high energy levels. Incorporating a variety of these foods into your meals ensures a spectrum of necessary nutrients that power up your body naturally.

Apart from nutrient density, understanding macronutrients—proteins, fats, and carbohydrates—is equally important in creating balanced meals. Each plays a unique role in fueling the body. Carbohydrates are often considered the body's preferred source of fuel because they convert easily into glucose, which cells use for energy. Proteins, found in lean meats, beans, and nuts, help repair tissues and build muscle. This gives you long-term stamina by supporting muscle maintenance and growth. Fats, meanwhile, should not be sidelined. Healthy fats from avocados, nuts, and olive oil are valuable for brain health and offer a concentrated source of energy. By balancing these macronutrients in every meal, you create not only satisfying dishes but also ones that release energy steadily throughout the day, avoiding sudden fatigue or lethargy.

Now let's talk about meal timing strategies. How often you eat can also play a crucial role in energy management. Regular eating patterns, where smaller, balanced meals or snacks are consumed every few hours, prevent the highs and lows typically associated with large meals followed by long intervals without food. This approach keeps blood sugar stable and helps avoid energy dips. Incorporating healthy snacks such as a handful of almonds or an apple with peanut butter between meals can provide a quick boost while ensuring that your overall nutritional intake supports optimal energy levels.

In terms of micronutrients, their impact on energy is profound but often underestimated. Micronutrients encompass vitamins and minerals that are fundamental in energy production processes. For example, B vitamins, iron, and magnesium are critical players in converting food into usable energy. B vitamins act as co-enzymes that assist in metabolizing carbohydrates, fats, and proteins. Iron carries oxygen to cells, which is integral for sustained energy and preventing anemia, a common cause of fatigue. Magnesium aids in the synthesis of ATP, which is essentially the energy currency within our cells. Deficiencies in any of these micronutrients can lead to noticeable drops in energy, resulting in constant tiredness and a lack of motivation.

To maintain optimum energy levels, assessing your diet for these essential nutrients is beneficial. This might involve adjusting your food choices or even consulting with a healthcare provider if you're experiencing persistent fatigue. By filling any gaps in your nutrient intake, you'll likely experience a remarkable improvement in how energized you feel day-to-day.

Craft a Sleep Routine That Revitalizes You

Getting enough sleep is crucial for feeling energetic and ready to tackle the day. Understanding sleep cycles can help optimize restfulness by aligning our schedules with these natural rhythms. Sleep is composed of cycles, each lasting about

90 minutes, comprising both REM (rapid eye movement) and non-REM sleep phases. While REM sleep is associated with dreaming and cognitive functions, non-REM sleep aids physical recovery and immune function. Targeting wake times that coincide with the end of a 90-minute cycle ensures waking up during lighter phases of sleep, making mornings more refreshing.

Most people don't realize how much their surroundings can affect their sleep quality. A conducive sleep environment makes all the difference. Start by ensuring your bedroom is dark; light interference can disrupt the production of melatonin, the hormone responsible for regulating sleep. Using blackout curtains or an eye mask can be immensely helpful. Silence is golden when it comes to quality sleep—minimizing disruptive sounds through earplugs or white noise machines can create a tranquil atmosphere, free from disturbances. The temperature in your room also plays a significant role. Keeping your room cool, around 65 degrees Fahrenheit, facilitates better sleep as it mimics the body's natural drop in core temperature as it prepares for slumber.

Creating a nightly wind-down routine is another pillar of good sleep hygiene. Before going to bed, engage in calming activities that signal your body it's time to relax and prepare for sleep. Allocate at least 30 minutes for winding down. This could include listening to soft music, doing some gentle yoga stretches, or reading a book under dim lighting. It's essential to establish consistency in this routine as repeating the same relaxing activities nightly helps condition your body to recognize bedtime cues. Dimming lights an hour before your intended sleep time enhances melatonin production, further signaling to your body that it's time to rest.

Modern life often causes anxiety and stress, which can severely impact sleep quality. Mindfulness techniques provide excellent tools for relaxation and setting the stage for restful sleep. Meditation has been shown to reduce stress levels significantly, offering a calm mind ready for sleep. Techniques such as guided imagery or progressive muscle relaxation can ease tension and promote tranquility. Mindful breathing—focusing on slow, deliberate breaths—shifts focus away from stressors, helping quiet the mind. Engaging in mindfulness practices regularly not only benefits bedtime but results in long-lasting improvements in overall mental health and well-being.

Incorporate Stretching and Movement Breaks in Your Routine

Regular movement and stretching are vital for maintaining high energy levels throughout the day. The modern lifestyle, with its increasing reliance on technology and sedentary habits, often leads to stagnation in our bodies, which can drain our energy and affect our productivity. To counter this, incorporating regular stretching into daily routines is beneficial not just for physical health but also for mental sharpness. Stretching helps improve blood circulation, which ensures that oxygen and nutrients are effectively delivered to your muscles and brain. This, in turn, enhances mental alertness and focus, making it easier to tackle tasks with clarity and efficiency.

Imagine sitting for hours at a desk; over time, your muscles become tense, your posture worsens, and your mind starts to wander. A simple stretch or two can break this cycle, alleviate muscle tension, and refocus your mind. It's akin to rebooting a sluggish computer to make it run smoothly again. Implementing quick stretching exercises every hour can transform how you feel and work, keeping both muscle stiffness and mental fatigue at bay.

An effective way to ensure these breaks happen regularly is by using methods like the Pomodoro Technique. This approach involves working for a set period, usually 25 minutes, followed by a short break. During this break, instead of reaching for your phone or scrolling through social media, try engaging in light physical activities or stretches. This intentional pause not only combats fatigue but also refreshes your mental state, leading to increased productivity and creativity when you return to your tasks.

For many, the idea of exercise might conjure up images of long workouts at the gym or rigorous training sessions, but it doesn't have to be so. Finding enjoyable activities is key to maintaining consistent physical activity. Consider what brings joy to your life—perhaps it's dancing around your living room to your favorite tunes, playing a sport with friends, or even taking a leisurely walk in the park. These activities don't just keep you physically active; they inject fun and excitement into your day. Joyful movement releases endorphins, the body's natural mood lifters, contributing to sustained energy levels and enhancing overall well-being.

Mindfulness in movement adds another layer of benefit, integrating both physical and mental aspects of rejuvenation. Practices such as yoga and tai chi emphasize not only the physical postures but also the mental discipline and awareness of breath. Through mindful movement, we're encouraged to listen to our bodies and minds, recognizing stress points and shifting our energy flow intentionally. Yoga, particularly, offers a blend of flexibility, strength, and meditation that can invigorate the spirit and calm the mind, making it an ideal practice for individuals seeking balanced energy restoration.

Incorporating mindful movement into your routine isn't about mastering complex poses but about finding stillness and balance within movement. Even in the midst of a chaotic schedule, dedicating a few moments to stretch and breathe deeply can reset your mindset and renew your vigor.

It's important to remember that the ultimate goal of these practices is not perfection but consistency. Developing a routine that includes scheduled movement and stretching fosters a lifestyle conducive to maintaining energy levels, no matter the demands of daily life. Regular breaks throughout the day, coupled with movement that sparks joy, create a framework where energy is continuously replenished rather than depleted.

Engagement with colleagues in a friendly sports match, attending a yoga class, or simply choosing to take the stairs instead of the elevator are small, everyday choices that contribute to an active life. When prioritizing movement, we're investing in ourselves, ensuring that we meet each day's challenges with vitality and enthusiasm.

To truly harness the benefits of regular movement and stretching, consider tracking your progress. Whether through a simple journal or a fitness app, monitoring how these changes affect your energy and mood can be motivating. This self-awareness helps reinforce positive habits and highlights the tangible impact of staying active.

Hydrate Consistently Throughout the Day

In navigating the ups and downs of adulthood, it's crucial to understand how something as simple as staying hydrated can have a profound impact on your energy levels and cognitive function. When we talk about hydration, we're referring not just to drinking water, but also understanding our individual needs and ensuring we meet them. This understanding supports everything from our physical vitality to mental clarity—a key focus for anyone juggling responsibilities like work, school, and social commitments.

First, let's explore how individual hydration needs vary based on activities. Whether you're hitting the gym, studying for exams, or working long hours, each activity demands different fluid levels. For instance, athletes often lose fluids rapidly and need more than the standard recommendation to replenish their bodies. On the other hand, those engaged in less physically demanding tasks might require less but still need to maintain consistent intake. Recognizing these variations helps ensure that you're giving your body the right amount of fluids it needs to function optimally. This approach prevents fatigue commonly associated with dehydration and keeps your energy levels stable throughout the day.

Dehydration is a silent thief that affects both our body and mind. Even a slight dip in fluid intake can lead to noticeable symptoms like tiredness, reduced memory, and poor concentration. According to *The National Council on Aging*, losing as little as 2% of body fluid can negatively impact brain performance, including mood and reaction times. This makes proper hydration even more important for older adults who might already face challenges in maintaining cognitive function. For young adults and college students, staying hydrated could mean fewer moments of struggling to concentrate during late-night study sessions or mid-afternoon slumps at work. Ensuring adequate fluid intake throughout the day not only maintains baseline energy levels but also sharpens cognitive capabilities, allowing you to stay focused and perform better.

Now, let's delve into the role of fluid-rich foods. Incorporating fruits and vegetables into your diet can significantly boost your hydration status while also infusing your body with vital nutrients. Foods like watermelon, cucumbers, and oranges are high in water content and provide essential vitamins and minerals that support overall health. Including these in meals or snacks is an easy way to enhance hydration without constantly reaching for a drink. These options not only hydrate but also contribute to feeling fuller and more satisfied, which aligns well with maintaining a balanced diet and managing weight effectively.

While plain water is undoubtedly a source of hydration, there are creative ways to make drinking water more appealing, encouraging regular intake. For those who find drinking water a chore, flavored water offers an exciting alternative. Add slices of lemon, mint leaves, or berries to your water for a refreshing twist. Not only do these infusions add flavor, but they may also introduce additional nutrients. Moreover, engaging in hydration challenges with friends or colleagues can turn maintaining hydration into a fun and motivating activity. Setting daily goals or creating reminders using mobile apps can encourage consistent fluid intake, transforming a mundane task into an enjoyable routine.

Beyond just fulfilling a biological need, paying attention to hydration has extensive benefits for emotional well-being and productivity. When you're adequately hydrated, your body operates smoothly, reducing unnecessary stress and allowing you to tackle tasks with a clear mind. Young professionals will find this particularly beneficial in managing workplace challenges with ease and efficiency. Furthermore, being well-hydrated ensures that your brain functions optimally, enabling you to engage fully in social interactions and build meaningful relationships without the fog of fatigue clouding your mind.

Staying hydrated doesn't just improve your current state; it sets a foundation for long-term health. As you establish habits around hydration, you're investing in future vitality and resilience. This becomes especially evident when considering the adverse long-term effects of chronic dehydration, such as kidney stones or urinary tract infections, which can be painful and disruptive. By developing a mindset that prioritizes hydration today, you're taking a proactive step towards safeguarding your health tomorrow.

Find Activities that Invigorate Rather than Exhaust You

In the pursuit of boosting your energy levels, choosing the right activities can make all the difference. The key is to select those that invigorate and inspire you rather than exhaust and drain your vitality. Identifying what truly excites you is a great starting point. Engage in introspection to find activities that align with your interests and passions. Whether it's painting, hiking, or playing a musical instrument, discovering these personal interests can lead to experiences that energize and motivate you.

When you participate in activities that resonate with your personality and desires, you often find yourself more engaged and enthusiastic. This engagement is crucial because it can convert what might otherwise be a tiring endeavor into something refreshingly uplifting. For instance, if you love being outdoors, a long walk in nature might provide a sense of rejuvenation that sitting indoors cannot. By aligning activities with personal interests, you're more likely to sustain your energy and maintain longer-lasting enthusiasm.

Equally important is setting boundaries on exhaustive tasks. Many people fall into the trap of overcommitting themselves, leading to burnout and fatigue. Understanding where to draw the line is vital in preserving your energy for pursuits that bring you joy. Instead of filling every hour with things to do, focus on what genuinely matters to you and allocate time accordingly. Avoid taking on more than you can handle by prioritizing tasks and scheduling breaks for relaxation and reflection. This approach not only prevents exhaustion but also leaves room for enjoyable activities that recharge your spirit.

Balancing tasks and creating space for enjoyable pursuits requires discipline and foresight. It's about knowing when to say no and protecting your time for activities that nurture you. Setting boundaries involves recognizing the signs of fatigue and stress and making a conscious decision to avoid reaching breaking points. Consider delegating tasks when possible or seeking help to lighten your load. By doing so, you preserve your mental and physical resources, allowing you to engage in activities that bring fulfillment and happiness.

Cultivating joy in everyday routines is another way to transform mundane tasks into sources of energy. Injecting creativity into daily chores can make them less tedious and more enjoyable. For example, listening to your favorite music while cleaning the house or turning meal preparation into a fun cooking experiment can elevate your mood and boost your energy. It's about finding small ways to make routine tasks feel special and rewarding.

This approach doesn't just make tasks more bearable; it elevates your overall well-being by adding excitement to the ordinary. Creativity stimulates the mind and invites positivity, reducing the feeling of drudgery associated with everyday responsibilities. When you regularly practice infusing joy into daily activities, you create an environment that consistently supports your energy levels and enhances your quality of life. By embracing spontaneity and innovative thinking, you can transform even the most routine duties into opportunities for revitalization.

Creating a personalized energizing plan can provide a structured pathway to incorporating revitalizing activities into your life. Begin by assessing your current lifestyle and determining where changes can be made. Identify activities that you enjoy and schedule them into your routine. A personalized plan should consider the balance between work, leisure, and rest. Make realistic goals and start small, gradually building up to more ambitious activities as your energy levels improve.

Having a structured plan ensures that you stay committed to engaging in activities that uplift you. It provides clarity and focus, allowing you to prioritize self-care and personal growth. The plan acts as a roadmap to guide you through the process of integrating energizing activities into your life, ensuring that you take deliberate and consistent steps toward enhancing your vitality. Consistently revisit and adjust your plan to accommodate changes in interests or lifestyle, ensuring that it remains relevant and effective.

Additionally, consider collaborating with friends or loved ones who share similar interests, as this can add a social dimension to your plan. Engaging in group activities not only promotes accountability but also brings additional joy and motivation through shared experiences. Having a supportive network encourages you to stay on track and to explore new activities that you may not have considered independently.

It's essential to remember that incorporating energizing activities into your life is not a one-size-fits-all solution. Each person's situation is unique, and it's important to tailor your approach to fit your individual needs and circumstances. Be open to experimenting with different activities and observe how they impact your energy levels and overall enjoyment. Over time, you'll develop a deeper understanding of what works best for you, enabling you to craft a lifestyle that consistently boosts your energy and enhances your well-being.

Bringing It All Together

As we wrap up this chapter, we've taken a journey through various strategies that can significantly boost your energy levels. From the foods you consume to the way you move and rest, each element plays a crucial role in helping you feel more vibrant and alive. We've explored how choosing nutrient-dense foods ensures a steady release of energy throughout the day, while understanding the importance of micronutrients in maintaining vitality. Sleep, too, is a cornerstone of feeling refreshed, with tips on creating an environment and routine that supports quality rest. By bringing movement into your daily life, whether through stretching or engaging activities, you not only enhance physical flexibility but also invigorate your mental well-being. Consistent hydration remains an unsung hero, underscoring its vital role in supporting cognitive function and overall energy.

The chapter's insights aim to empower young adults, college students, and professionals alike to craft a lifestyle that supports their unique energy needs. Each strategy offers practical, manageable steps tailored to fit into the busy lives of those navigating adulthood's complexities. Remember to find joy in what you do—whether through hobbies that ignite your passion or small tweaks to everyday tasks that bring satisfaction. It's about making conscious choices that prioritize balance and self-care. As you integrate these practices into your life, you'll likely notice improved mood, focus, and endurance, setting a foundation for a healthier, more fulfilling future.

9

Effective Communication Skills

Enhance Relationships through Active Listening and Expressed Empathy

Building strong relationships often hinges on our ability to truly listen and empathize with those around us. Active listening and expressed empathy aren't just buzzwords; they are fundamental skills that foster deeper connections and understanding in our interactions. Imagine a friend pouring their heart out about a tough day, and instead of merely hearing them, you actually engage, making them feel supported and valued. This sort of interaction can transform the dynamics of any relationship, whether personal or professional. By focusing on how we communicate, we unlock the potential for more meaningful connections, making everyday exchanges more impactful and rewarding.

In this chapter, you'll explore the nuances of active listening and empathy as cornerstones of effective communication. We'll delve into recognizing non-verbal cues that accompany spoken words, such as body language and facial expressions, which often convey more than verbal messages alone. You'll also discover techniques like maintaining eye contact and respecting personal space, all while understanding cultural differences that can affect these interactions. Moreover, the practice of articulating emotions clearly and constructively will be discussed, helping you manage emotions and reduce misunderstandings. These insights will equip you to deepen your relationships, ensuring your message aligns with your intentions and is received positively by others.

Learn the Art of Non-Verbal Communication

Understanding non-verbal cues is essential for improving communication and building deeper relationships. In any interaction, these silent signals can speak volumes, often conveying more than words themselves. They act as a language of their own, rich with emotion and meaning. As young adults navigating the complexities of adulthood, mastering this form of communication can significantly deepen connections with friends, family, and colleagues.

Starting with body language, it's crucial to acknowledge how gestures and posture communicate your internal state. When you stand tall with your shoulders back, you exude confidence. This posture not only affects how others perceive you but also influences how you feel about yourself. For instance, in a job interview, maintaining an open and upright posture can project assurance, enhancing your chances of making a positive impression. On the flip side, slouching or avoiding eye contact might suggest insecurity or disinterest. Understanding these nuances allows you to adjust your body language to better suit the situation, ensuring your non-verbal cues align with your verbal messages.

Facial expressions are another vital component of non-verbal communication. A genuine smile, for instance, can instantly foster trust and warmth, opening the door for authentic interactions. Think about meeting someone new: a sincere smile can serve as an invitation, encouraging them to engage more openly. Conversely, forced or inauthentic expressions can create barriers, leading to mistrust or skepticism. Studies have shown that people are remarkably adept at distinguishing between genuine and fake smiles, which underscores the importance of authenticity in facial expressions. Smiling authentically, even in stressful situations, can diffuse tension and convey approachability, paving the way for stronger connections.

Eye contact holds its own power in non-verbal communication. It signifies attentiveness and respect, forming the foundation of effective interaction. By maintaining appropriate eye contact—that is, steady yet not overpowering—you uphold a level of engagement that speaks volumes about your interest and involvement in the conversation. Consider a classroom setting: a student who maintains eye contact with a professor is perceived as engaged and responsive, potentially enhancing their learning experience. However, it's important to be mindful of cultural differences, as direct eye contact may be interpreted differently across cultures. Therefore, balancing eye contact with cultural awareness can enhance mutual understanding and acceptance.

Proxemics, or the study of personal space, plays a significant role in shaping our interactions. The physical distance we maintain during conversations subtly communicates comfort levels and relational closeness. For example, standing too close to someone who isn't familiar can cause discomfort, while too much distance from a friend or loved one might signal disengagement or detachment. Understanding these spatial dynamics can help manage boundaries effectively, ensuring that interactions remain comfortable and respectful. Being aware of personal space norms is particularly useful in professional settings where misjudging proxemics might lead to misunderstandings or unintentional offenses.

While each of these components—body language, facial expressions, eye contact, and proxemics—functions independently, they collectively enrich the tapestry of communication. Recognizing their interplay provides a fuller understanding of both what is being communicated and how it is received. Misinterpretation of non-verbal signals can lead to unnecessary conflict; therefore, it's beneficial to become adept at reading these cues accurately. Just as importantly, honing your ability to control and express your non-verbal cues can fortify your message, ensuring clarity and reinforcing your intent.

In practical terms, improving your non-verbal communication involves practice and mindfulness. Start by observing your own non-verbal habits. Notice how your posture changes depending on your emotional state. Are you crossing your arms when you're upset? Or maybe your voice softens when you're feeling empathetic? Self-awareness is the first step in transforming your non-verbal communication skills. It allows you to recognize patterns and make conscious decisions about changing behaviors that may not serve you well.

Similarly, observe how others around you employ non-verbal cues. Pay attention to what someone's facial expressions reveal when they are telling a story. Are their eyes lighting up with excitement? Is there a certain gesture they keep repeating that emphasizes their words? By becoming more attentive to these details, you naturally become more attuned to the feelings and intentions behind people's actions, which enhances your empathetic abilities.

Another valuable skill is recognizing incongruent non-verbal cues. Sometimes, verbal communication may say one thing, while the body says another. For example, if someone claims they're fine but avoid eye contact and fidget nervously, it might indicate underlying issues that need addressing. Being able to identify such discrepancies equips you with the tools to probe deeper, fostering more honest and meaningful exchanges.

Lastly, always remember to ask before assuming. Non-verbal communication can vary widely across different cultures and individual personalities. What might be considered a sign of respect in one culture could be seen as impolite in another. Open dialogue about these interpretations ensures mutual understanding and avoids miscommunication. Something as simple as confirming, "I noticed you seemed quiet in the meeting; is there anything you'd like to share?" can prevent assumptions and open paths for clearer communication (Cherry, 2023).

Develop Skills to Articulate Emotions Clearly and Constructively

Being able to express emotions effectively fosters understanding and mitigates misunderstandings in relationships. It's not uncommon for emotions to be misinterpreted or suppressed, leading to confusion between individuals. By honing the skill of emotional expression, you can cultivate deeper connections with others.

Identifying Emotions is the first significant step. It might seem simple, but accurately pinpointing feelings is often more challenging than it appears. Consider moments when you've responded to someone with irritation, only to realize later that the root was actually stress or fatigue. Understanding your own emotions helps in conveying them clearly to others. For instance, saying "I'm feeling overwhelmed" rather than lashing out about a trivial issue allows the other person to understand your state of mind better. Encouraging conversations around specific emotions can also help both parties feel more understood and less judged.

Next comes the Use of 'I' Statements. This tool is incredibly effective in reducing defensiveness during discussions. When faced with conflict, we might instinctively use "you" statements, like "You never listen!" which can set a confrontational tone. Instead, rephrasing this as "I feel unheard sometimes" shifts the focus to your personal experience rather than blaming the other person. This method encourages open dialogue by ensuring that each party feels they're being spoken with rather than at. Moreover, using 'I' statements requires you to take responsibility for your feelings, reinforcing self-awareness.

Constructive Language works hand in hand with 'I' statements to promote positive communication. By consciously choosing words that frame the conversation optimistically, you create an environment where solutions are possible. Suppose you're discussing a recurring issue, like balancing chores with a partner. A statement like "I appreciate when we work together on tasks; it makes me feel supported" gently nudges the conversation towards cooperation without apportioning blame. This approach nurtures mutual respect and understanding, essential components of a healthy relationship.

Effective Timing is crucial in emotion expression. Navigating emotional conversations when you're calm rather than in the heat of the moment enhances clarity and empathy. Reacting immediately during a heated moment, such as a disagreement, can lead to regrettable exchanges. Instead, allowing yourself to cool down before expressing how you feel increases the likelihood of a positive outcome. If something bothers you during a meeting or social gathering, for instance, waiting until later to address it will likely prevent unnecessary tension. This doesn't mean avoidance; it's about choosing the best time when both parties can engage constructively.

Consider the example of a young adult dealing with stress from school or work. They might come home feeling frustrated and unintentionally direct their pent-up emotions towards friends or family. Identification of emotions here would look like acknowledging "I feel stressed because of my workload". Using an 'I' statement, they could communicate, "I need some quiet time to unwind and focus on my projects." Constructive language might involve suggesting, "Let's find a time this weekend to hang out after I catch up on some work," facilitating understanding and collaboration. By timing these expressions after calming activities, like a short walk or meditation, they significantly improve comprehension and reduce friction.

In a professional setting, mastering these skills can make a young employee stand out. Imagine handling a misunderstanding with a coworker. Identifying emotions lets the employee recognize that anxiety about deadlines is affecting their interactions. They might use an 'I' statement, such as "I feel anxious about our project timeline," rather than accusing a colleague of inefficiency. Constructive language could follow: "Can we coordinate our tasks to ensure we're aligned?" This turns potential conflict into collaboration. Expressing these thoughts once they've taken a moment to compose their thoughts, perhaps after consulting a mentor or following a deep-breathing exercise, leads to clearer and more productive communication.

Through these practical examples, it's evident that emotional expression isn't merely about airing grievances or sharing joy—it's about building bridges. In personal, academic, and professional spheres, effective emotional expression empowers individuals to navigate complex interactions gracefully. As you practice identifying your feelings, crafting 'I' statements, employing constructive language, and choosing the right moments for conversations, you'll find that your relationships deepen, becoming more resilient and fulfilling.

Practice Active Listening During Conversations

In today's fast-paced world, communication often happens on the fly, leaving relationships to navigate through misunderstandings or assumptions. However, active listening is a skill that can change this dynamic, leading to more meaningful conversations and deeper connections. Most people think they are good listeners. But how often do we find ourselves distracted during conversations, only giving half our attention? The importance of full attention cannot be overstated. When someone is speaking, offering your undivided attention eliminates distractions and demonstrates respect. It builds a foundation of trust, showing that you value what the other person has to say. Imagine a scenario where you're meeting a friend for coffee. They start talking about their latest project, and instead of checking your phone or gazing out the window, you focus solely on them. This small act of removing distractions shows your commitment to the conversation, making the other person feel valued and understood.

Reflective listening takes this engagement one step further. By paraphrasing what the speaker has said, you confirm your participation in the dialogue. This technique not only clarifies your understanding but also reassures the speaker that their message was received as intended. For instance, after listening to your friend discuss their project, you might respond with something like, "So, you're saying the new project is both exciting and challenging for you?" This reflection serves multiple purposes: it confirms your comprehension, shows empathy, and encourages the speaker to elaborate on their thoughts.

Another vital component of active listening is asking clarifying questions. Sometimes, assuming we understand leads to miscommunication. Follow-up questions can bridge this gap, enhancing comprehension by inviting the speaker to provide more context or details. Let's say your friend mentions some difficulties they're facing at work; instead of jumping to conclusions, you might ask, "Could you explain more about the challenges you're encountering?" Such inquiries prevent assumptions and ensure you truly grasp the speaker's perspective.

Providing non-verbal feedback, such as nods or affirmations, plays a crucial role in reinforcing verbal communication. These gestures show that you are present in the moment and encourage the speaker to continue sharing openly. Imagine sitting across from your friend, listening attentively while nodding occasionally as they speak. These subtle cues convey that you are genuinely interested in what they have to say, fostering an atmosphere of trust and openness. Studies have shown that these non-verbal signals are integral to effective communication, facilitating smoother interactions (Weger et al., 2014).

The benefits of honing active listening skills extend beyond personal relationships. In professional settings, especially those demanding precision, such as healthcare, mastering these techniques can lead to improved outcomes. Communication breakdowns in high-stakes environments can have serious consequences. For example, a doctor who actively listens to a patient's concerns will likely make more accurate diagnoses and deliver better care. Active listening helps in building rapport with colleagues and increases team cohesion, ultimately reducing stress and enhancing workplace efficiency (Tennant et al., 2023).

For young adults, particularly those entering the workforce or managing academic pressures, active listening is a crucial tool. Navigating relationships, whether at work, school, or socially, requires clear and respectful communication. Attentive listening ensures you engage fully in each interaction, cultivating mutual respect and trust. College students and young professionals can apply these skills to manage emotions, reduce misunderstandings, and build networks that support their personal and professional growth.

Imagine being in a team meeting where everyone is eager to contribute ideas. By practicing active listening, you show respect to your peers' contributions, perhaps paraphrasing what they've said before adding your own insights. This approach sets a collaborative tone and endorses a culture of open communication. Furthermore, asking insightful questions elevates the discussion, demonstrating that you are invested in achieving the collective goals.

Active listening is more than just a nice-to-have skill—it's a necessity for effective communication. In moments where messages could be misconstrued due to cultural differences or language barriers, active listening serves as a powerful equalizer. Professionals equipped with these skills are better positioned to foster inclusive environments, bridging gaps that hinder understanding and cooperation.

For personal development, embracing active listening can be transformative. It encourages patience, empathy, and humility—qualities that strengthen relationships across all areas of life. Practicing mindfulness and focusing on the present are essential elements of this listening style, allowing individuals to connect with others authentically.

Although some may doubt the superiority of active listening over simple acknowledgments or advice-giving, research underscores its effectiveness in creating meaningful dialogues. While advice might shift focus away from the speaker's perspective, active listening keeps the conversation centered on understanding. This practice leads to higher levels of satisfaction in conversations, laying the groundwork for stronger bonds and reduced conflict (Weger et al., 2014).

Apply the Concept of 'I' Statements to Express Needs

In relationships, effective communication is pivotal, and using 'I' statements can be a game-changer. Instead of sparking defensiveness, this technique invites open dialogue and understanding. Let's delve into how 'I' statements function and their impact on relationships.

One significant advantage of 'I' statements is their ability to de-escalate conflicts. When disagreements arise, people tend to adopt defensive stances, which can intensify the situation. By focusing on one's feelings rather than assigning blame, 'I' statements create a safer space for discussion. For instance, saying "I feel overwhelmed when deadlines pile up" instead of "You never help with deadlines" shifts the conversation from accusation to collaboration. This approach lowers defenses and fosters constructive dialogue, allowing both parties to address underlying concerns without feeling attacked.

Another crucial benefit of using 'I' statements is their role in building emotional intelligence. Emotional intelligence involves recognizing and managing one's emotions while also empathizing with others. 'I' statements enhance these skills by encouraging individuals to own their emotions. By articulating feelings clearly, individuals practice self-awareness and accountability. This not only improves personal growth but also strengthens relational skills. Expressing emotions responsibly creates an environment where partners feel heard and understood, paving the way for emotional connections that are vital for healthy relationships.

Clarity in communication is another strength of 'I' statements. Misunderstandings often arise from assumptions and ambiguous exchanges. When individuals express their feelings explicitly, they minimize the room for misinterpretation. Clear messages prevent confusion, enabling both parties to understand perspectives better. For example, saying "I feel hurt when plans change last minute" provides specific insights into the speaker's experience, reducing the chances of a misconstrued message. This clarity enhances mutual understanding and promotes honest conversations.

Incorporating 'I' statements into conversations also models vulnerability. Sharing personal emotions and needs requires openness, which can foster deeper emotional bonds between partners. Vulnerability involves taking risks in revealing one's authentic self, which, although challenging, can lead to stronger, more genuine relationships. An example could be expressing, "I feel anxious about our current situation," which invites empathy and encourages the partner to reciprocate with support and understanding. This openness cultivates trust, creating a foundation for emotional intimacy.

While 'I' statements offer numerous benefits, it is essential to consider some challenges and nuances associated with their use. Overreliance on 'I' statements can make communication seem rigid or rehearsed. It's important to maintain authenticity and adapt the technique as needed. Additionally, 'I' statements can be misused to disguise blame (e.g., "I feel like you're being inconsiderate") rather than genuinely expressing personal feelings. Practicing honest reflection before speaking helps ensure these statements reflect true emotions and needs.

Moreover, cultural differences can influence the receptivity of 'I' statements. In some cultures, direct expression of personal feelings may be less socially acceptable, requiring sensitivity and adaptation to varying norms. It's important to respect different communication styles while finding common ground that respects both partners' preferences.

Implementing 'I' statements effectively often begins with practice in low-stakes situations. Starting with everyday interactions allows individuals to become comfortable with the technique, making its use more natural during conflicts. Reflecting before speaking is also crucial; taking a moment to identify emotions and needs ensures genuine communication. Specificity is key—focusing on particular behaviors or situations rather than generalizing helps convey clear messages. Encouraging partners to use 'I' statements as well can establish a mutual language of personal responsibility and emotional honesty.

Implement Feedback Gracefully and Effectively

Navigating the complexities of giving and receiving feedback is an essential skill in deepening relationships, particularly among young adults and professionals. By understanding how to approach criticism constructively, we open doors to more meaningful and effective communication.

Constructive criticism is a cornerstone for building strong, resilient interactions. When criticism is framed positively, it becomes an opportunity for dialogue rather than confrontation. For instance, instead of pointing out flaws directly, commenting on areas of potential improvement in a supportive manner can foster openness. Using language that focuses on specific behaviors and outcomes rather than personal attributes helps avoid defensiveness and promotes a collaborative atmosphere. This positive framing allows all parties to engage without fear of judgment or hostility, setting the stage for productive conversations.

Receiving feedback gracefully is equally crucial. Viewing feedback as an opportunity for growth requires a mindset shift from seeing criticism as a personal attack to valuing it as valuable input. It's important to manage initial emotional reactions; take a moment to process feedback before responding, as this ensures that communication remains composed and respectful. Ask clarifying questions if needed, showing genuine interest in understanding the perspective offered. By maintaining composure, individuals can preserve and even strengthen their relationships, turning potentially negative experiences into constructive exchanges.

Creating an open culture is fundamental for fostering honest communication and trust among peers. An environment where feedback is regularly exchanged builds a sense of security and mutual respect. When individuals feel safe to speak candidly, they are more likely to express thoughts that could contribute significantly to personal and communal growth. Encouraging feedback through regular check-ins or feedback sessions can help instill this culture. Leadership also plays a pivotal role by modeling openness and receptivity, thereby inspiring others to follow suit. In such environments, feedback becomes a routine aspect of interaction, normalizing its practice and importance.

Additionally, follow-up communication is vital to sustaining the benefits of feedback. Continuously engaging with the feedback received demonstrates a commitment to improvement. Whether you're applying changes based on feedback or offering additional support to help someone understand your perspective, reaching out after initial discussions reinforces the ongoing nature of development. Following up shows that feedback is not a one-time event but part of a continuous journey toward betterment. This engagement keeps communication channels open, further strengthening the relationship by highlighting a collective investment in each other's success.

For young adults, especially those transitioning into professional environments, mastering these elements can make a significant difference. The ability to both offer and accept feedback gracefully is invaluable in navigating workplace dynamics and building lasting friendships. Understanding the impact of constructive criticism can transform how individuals perceive and participate in conversations about personal and professional growth.

To illustrate, consider a scenario where a team member receives feedback on a project presentation. Instead of focusing on areas that fell short, their colleague highlights strengths, followed by suggestions for enhancement. The recipient might initially feel defensive but chooses to listen actively, asking questions to refine their understanding. By reflecting on the feedback later and implementing changes, not only does the quality of future presentations improve, but the relationship between colleagues strengthens thanks to this positive exchange.

This cycle of giving and receiving feedback serves as a powerful tool for personal development and relationship building. By consciously practicing constructive criticism, welcoming input with grace, fostering an open culture, and ensuring consistent follow-up communication, individuals can significantly enhance their interpersonal skills. These practices encourage a cycle of continuous improvement, benefiting both personal and professional spheres.

Summary and Reflections

In this chapter, we've explored the vital role communication skills play in crafting stronger connections with those around us. From understanding non-verbal cues like body language and eye contact to expressing emotions clearly through 'I' statements and practicing active listening, these tools are integral to enhancing our interactions. As we navigate through work, academic settings, or personal relationships, recognizing the power of these skills helps us communicate more effectively and fosters mutual respect and empathy.

By honing these techniques, we not only improve how we relate to others but also bolster our own emotional intelligence. Whether it's being mindful of cultural differences in communication styles or showing vulnerability by sharing our feelings, each step enriches our relational tapestry. As young adults and professionals, mastering these skills equips us with the confidence to handle various challenges life throws our way, paving the path for deeper relationships and a fulfilling, well-rounded lifestyle.

10

Fostering Deep Connections

uilding and Maintaining Meaningful Relationships
Building and maintaining meaningful relationships
involves thoughtful actions that nurture deeper
connections with the people closest to us. In today's fast-paced
world, it can be easy to lose sight of what's important amidst
our busy schedules and numerous distractions. However,
making a conscious effort to prioritize time with loved ones
can have lasting impacts on both our personal happiness
and emotional health. By taking intentional steps towards
fostering these bonds, we not only enrich our own lives but also
contribute to the well-being and fulfillment of those around us.
This chapter offers insights into how simple, yet purposeful
actions can transform our interactions into powerful sources
of support and joy.

Throughout this chapter, we will explore practical approaches
to strengthen ties with friends and family through genuine
efforts. From scheduling regular quality time to openly embracing each other's unique traits, we delve into the vari-

ous facets that make relationships thrive in unpredictable times. We'll discuss how shared experiences and simple rituals create lasting memories, while also examining the importance of adapting technology to maintain connections over long distances. Furthermore, embracing differences will be highlighted as a key element in creating an environment where everyone feels valued. Expect discussions on strategies to keep communication lines open despite hectic lifestyles, and discover why gratitude plays such a pivotal role in enhancing relationship satisfaction. These topics collectively aim to empower young adults, college students, and professionals alike, equipping them with useful tools to navigate the challenges of modern adult life while building enriching, enduring relationships.

Plan Regular Quality Time with Loved Ones

In today's fast-paced world, carving out dedicated time for relationships is more important than ever. Amidst the hustle and bustle of modern life, it can be challenging to prioritize our connections with loved ones. However, intentionally setting aside moments for friends and family not only strengthens these bonds but also enriches our lives with joy and fulfillment.

Shared activities form the cornerstone of these meaningful interactions. Participating in activities together helps foster deeper connections and create lasting memories. Whether it's embarking on a new adventure like hiking or revisiting a beloved tradition such as a weekly game night, these shared experiences bring people closer, enabling them to build inside jokes and shared stories that last a lifetime. The act of engaging in something together binds individuals, providing a platform where they can express themselves freely and learn more about each other in a relaxed environment.

Scheduled quality time creates a space where open communication flourishes. In the midst of hectic schedules, it's easy for genuine conversations to slip through the cracks. By deliberately planning moments to spend with loved ones, whether over a meal or during a leisurely walk, we open channels of communication that might otherwise remain closed. These moments offer the opportunity to discuss dreams, share concerns, and simply enjoy each other's company without the distractions of daily life. They become the bedrock of trust and understanding, crucial elements in any relationship.

Moreover, establishing rituals offers comfort and predictability, especially in turbulent times. Rituals are not just repetitive acts; they are comforting anchors that ground us when everything else feels uncertain. For instance, having Sunday brunch with family or a monthly movie night with friends provides a sense of stability and rhythm. These rituals signal to our loved ones that amidst chaos, there's always this safe haven to return to. They remind us that no matter how tumultuous life gets, we have enduring traditions that hold us together.

Finding a balance between quantity and quality of time spent with loved ones enriches the dynamics of our relationships. While some may equate more time with better connections, it's often the quality that counts. Fifteen minutes of undivided attention can mean far more than an entire afternoon where everyone is distracted. It's essential to gauge what works best for each relationship, ensuring that the time spent is both meaningful and sufficient to maintain closeness. This balance requires mindfulness and adaptability, allowing room for spontaneous adventures while still honoring pre-established commitments.

To ensure that scheduled quality time truly serves its purpose, consider implementing some guiding principles. First, eliminate distractions. Put away electronic devices and focus solely on those you are spending time with. This level of attention shows respect and interest, making the time feel special and valuable (*Quality Time Love Language: 5 Ways to Strengthen Your Bond*, 2024). Planning activities collaboratively can also enhance the experience, transforming ordinary moments into extraordinary memories. Finally, be open to adjusting plans. Flexibility allows for spontaneous moments of connection, which can sometimes turn out to be the most cherished.

Creating rituals doesn't require grand gestures or elaborate plans. Even simple practices can bring immense comfort. Think of morning coffee catch-ups or evening walks—it's the regularity that matters. These moments provide structure and familiarity, acting as a beacon through life's unpredictable nature. Moreover, engaging in such rituals reinforces the notion that relationships deserve nurturing and continuity.

Leveraging technology can bridge the gap when physical proximity isn't possible. Video calls, shared playlists, or even virtual games make it easier to maintain connections across distances. Technology, when used thoughtfully, enhances communication rather than detracts from it. It provides tools that keep interactions alive, ensuring that distance doesn't dilute relationships.

Ultimately, dedicating time to nurture relationships is an investment in happiness and emotional well-being. It involves consciously choosing to slow down and prioritize the people who matter most. As we navigate the complexities of entering adulthood, juggling academic pressures, or tackling professional challenges, these relationships provide the support system we need. They offer solace and strength, reminding us that we are never alone in our journeys.

Embrace and Celebrate Personal Differences

Appreciating individual differences plays a vital role in building and maintaining meaningful relationships. It's an art that, when mastered, not only enriches but also deepens our connections with others. In this discussion, we'll delve into how diverse perspectives, celebrating uniqueness, creating safe spaces, and using differences for growth contribute to the quality of our relationships.

Having diverse perspectives is akin to adding more colors to a palette; it broadens the scope of our experiences and enriches discussions. When we engage with people who think differently, we open ourselves up to new ideas and solutions that we might not have considered otherwise. These exchanges can lead to more informed decisions and creative problem-solving. For example, working on a group project in college or collaborating on a work assignment often involves team members who bring different viewpoints. This diversity can lead to innovative approaches and outcomes that a single-minded perspective might overlook.

Celebrating uniqueness is essential in forging stronger bonds. Recognizing what makes each person special encourages appreciation rather than criticism or judgment. Our differences, whether they are cultural, personality-based, or involve interests, should be embraced as something that adds value to our lives. By choosing to celebrate these differences, we honor the individuality of those we care about, which can strengthen our personal connections. Take, for instance, a friendship where one friend loves baking and the other enjoys playing guitar. By sharing these unique skills and passions, they create a dynamic environment where both feel valued and understood. Encouraging young adults to see the beauty in such diversity aids in fostering deeper connections.

Creating safe spaces is another crucial element where vulnerability and trust are nurtured. Safe spaces allow individuals to express themselves freely without fear of judgment or ridicule. In relationships, feeling secure enough to share one's thoughts and emotions is fundamental for developing trust and closeness. When people know they won't be criticized for their unique traits or opinions, they are more likely to show their true selves, making relationships richer and more authentic. In professional settings, workplaces that promote inclusivity create environments where employees feel empowered to share ideas that may deviate from the norm, leading to innovation and collaboration. For college students, engaging in groups or clubs where varied backgrounds are welcomed can offer invaluable insights and friendships.

Using differences as catalysts for personal growth is perhaps one of the most powerful aspects of embracing diversity.

Differences challenge us to step out of our comfort zones, prompting self-reflection and growth. By interacting with people who hold different beliefs or values, we gain a broader understanding of the human experience, which can lead to a more profound empathy and maturity. A young professional who travels or engages with international colleagues might find that exposure to different cultures expands their worldview and enhances their adaptability in diverse environments—skills that are invaluable in today's globalized world.

To maximize the benefits of these differences in enriching relationships, consider adopting a mindset of curiosity and openness. Approach interactions with the intent to learn and understand, rather than to judge. It is pivotal to remember that accepting someone's differences does not equate to agreeing with them. Instead, it means respecting those differences and allowing space for them without feeling threatened. This mindset helps dissolve prejudices and fears that often arise from misunderstanding.

Furthermore, actively listening is a practical guideline that can help in appreciating individual differences. Listening involves not just hearing words but understanding the context and emotions behind them. By practicing active listening, we affirm the worth of the other person's perspective, enhancing mutual respect and trust. This approach is particularly beneficial in resolving conflicts or during difficult conversations, where acknowledgment of differing opinions can pave the way for compromise and understanding.

For those enticed by the idea of using differences as opportunities for exploration, seek experiences that expose you to varied perspectives. Whether it's through travel, reading books by diverse authors, or participating in community events, these activities can broaden your horizons and challenge preconceived notions. The journey toward appreciating and leveraging differences for personal and relational growth is ongoing and rewarding.

Show Appreciation and Gratitude Frequently

In building and maintaining meaningful relationships, gratitude plays an instrumental role in fostering deep connections with others. When we appreciate those around us, the dynamics of our relationships are elevated, creating a foundation for deeper satisfaction and interpersonal growth. The act of expressing gratitude signals to the other person that they are valued and respected, which significantly enhances the quality of these interactions. Appreciation has been shown to enhance relationship satisfaction by making both parties feel seen and acknowledged.

One significant way appreciation elevates relationships is through different methods of expressing gratitude. Imagine this: a simple thank you, a heartfelt note, or a small token of appreciation can have profound effects on the recipient. These expressions evoke meaningful reactions because they signify effort and recognition, two critical components in any strong relationship. According to Algoe and Zhaoyang (2015), such behaviorally expressed gratitude not only acts as a reinforcer for positive actions but also brings about psychological benefits for both the giver and receiver. For example, couples who regularly express gratitude report higher levels of satisfaction and connection than those who don't.

Creating a habit of expressing gratitude can involve some creative approaches. For instance, writing a daily appreciation note or sharing things you're thankful for during a meal can become cherished rituals. For those seeking practical ways to integrate gratitude into their lives, consider setting reminders to pause and reflect on what you're grateful for, or discussing three gratitudes with your partner at the end of each day. These practices help keep gratitude at the forefront of our minds, ensuring its continued presence in everyday interactions.

Modeling gratitude further encourages reciprocation within relationships. When one partner consistently shows appreciation, it often inspires the other to do the same, creating a positive feedback loop. This concept is supported by research indicating that gratitude within relationships functions as part of a dynamic interpersonal process (Algoe & Zhaoyang, 2015). By modeling grateful behavior, individuals subtly encourage those around them to adopt similar attitudes, thereby strengthening the bond between them.

Demonstrating appreciation doesn't have to be grand; subtle gestures like acknowledging someone's effort in a group project or thanking a friend for lending a listening ear can foster an environment where gratitude thrives. Similarly, celebrating small achievements together can enhance mutual appreciation, reinforcing the importance of support and encouragement in the relationship.

The transformational impact of regular gratitude extends

beyond just influencing individual interactions; it has a lasting effect on emotional dynamics. Regularly practicing gratitude reshapes how we perceive and react to situations, promoting emotional resilience and fostering a more optimistic outlook. This shift can have far-reaching implications on overall mental health and well-being, positioning gratitude as a powerful tool for young adults facing various life challenges.

Gratitude also helps combat the brain's tendency to focus on the negative, especially during challenging times. As outlined in Source 2, gratitude practices not only reinforce personal well-being but significantly enhance relational satisfaction by balancing out stressors with positive acknowledgment (Your, 2024). In effect, gratitude acts as a buffer against negativity, allowing individuals to maintain healthy, balanced perspectives even when faced with adversity.

Moreover, expressing gratitude in real-time can prevent relationship conflicts from escalating. Instead of letting grievances fester, openly appreciating your partner's efforts fosters understanding and de-escalates potential arguments. This proactive communication approach enhances the emotional safety within the relationship, encouraging openness and vulnerability.

Resolve Conflicts with a Focus on Understanding

Navigating through conflicts in relationships requires a thoughtful and strategic approach to communication. At the heart of resolving disagreements lies the art of constructive communication, which is an essential tool to foster understanding and empathy between individuals. By mastering certain techniques, not only can one resolve conflicts effectively, but also strengthen the bond shared with others.

Open communication acts as the foundation of any successful resolution strategy. When each person involved in a conflict openly and clearly communicates their needs and concerns, it becomes possible to bridge gaps in understanding. Often, misunderstandings or assumptions lead to misconceptions that fuel disagreements. By encouraging transparency and honesty in discussions, you pave the way for clearer perceptions and expectations. For instance, if tension arises due to differing views on how much time should be spent together, expressing these feelings candidly helps clarify intentions and desires, steering the conversation toward mutual understanding.

However, open communication isn't just about speaking; it's equally critical to focus on active listening. This involves genuinely paying attention to what the other person is saying, without jumping to conclusions or interrupting their train of thought. Active listening enhances connections by showing respect and consideration for the other's point of view. Maintaining eye contact, summarizing what the speaker said, and asking relevant questions demonstrate interest and promote deeper dialogue. It's more than just hearing words— it's about grasping the emotions and intents behind them. This connection fosters a sense of validation and respect, making conflict resolution more effective and compassionate.

Beyond immediate interaction, finding common ground is vital for reaching amicable solutions. Conflicts often stem from perceived differences in goals or values. During a disagreement, focusing on shared objectives rather than dwelling on opposing positions can shift the dynamic from adversarial to collaborative. This strategy reroutes the conversation towards finding mutually acceptable solutions. In workplace disagreements over project priorities, highlighting the team's collective goal can help refocus efforts productively. Identifying these overlaps encourages cooperation and aligns both parties' efforts towards an agreed-upon outcome, creating a win-win situation.

Decoding underlying emotions is another critical aspect of resolving conflicts. Every quarrel has emotional undercurrents that may not be immediately visible. Understanding these hidden feelings requires empathy—the ability to appreciate another's emotions from their perspective. Recognizing anger, frustration, or fear can provide insights into why someone reacts a certain way. For instance, frequent arguments about chores might not solely be about tasks, but perhaps about feeling undervalued or overwhelmed. By addressing these root emotions, you create room for empathy and healing, transforming potentially destructive conflicts into opportunities for growth and deeper understanding.

Approaching conflicts with an open mindset is essential. It sets the stage for effective communication by creating an atmosphere conducive to honest expression without fear of judgment. To achieve this, acknowledge that conflicts are natural and can lead to positive change when handled constructively. Entering a discussion with openness allows space for diverse perspectives, enriching the dialogue and helping both parties feel heard and respected. This practice encourages a culture of continuous improvement within relationships, where differences become avenues for learning rather than sources of division.

Guidelines serve as useful reminders in these scenarios: embracing open communication, practicing active listening, seeking common ground, and empathizing with underlying emotions can transform conflicts into powerful bonding experiences. When applied consistently, these strategies ensure that even the toughest conversations lead to strengthened relationships and enhanced mutual respect.

The ability to resolve conflicts constructively has far-reaching implications beyond the immediate relationship dynamics. For young adults and professionals, these skills translate into improved interactions in personal and professional spheres. Enhanced communication abilities contribute to a more harmonious social environment, reducing stress and fostering more meaningful connections. As young adults enter complex phases of life with multiple responsibilities, mastering these techniques provides valuable coping mechanisms to navigate challenges with confidence and composure.

Moreover, understanding and implementing conflict resolution strategies empower individuals with the emotional intelligence necessary to maintain equilibrium in varied situations. The ripple effect of skillful conflict management extends beyond single instances, establishing patterns of behavior that promote enduring peace and co-existence.

Practice Forgiveness as a Tool for Emotional Freedom

Forgiveness is an essential tool in building and maintaining meaningful relationships, offering profound opportunities for self-liberation and emotional growth. At its core, forgiveness allows individuals to release themselves from the burdens of past grievances and embrace a healthier state of mind. By forgiving, one can break free from the cycle of negativity that anger, hatred, and bitterness often create (JONES, 2024). This liberation fosters personal development, encouraging self-reflection and empathy which are crucial components in enhancing interpersonal bonds.

Understanding the role of forgiveness begins with acknowledging the pain caused by others or oneself. This acknowledgment doesn't mean you condone the actions that hurt you, but it's a necessary step in healing. Allowing yourself to recognize this pain enables you to understand the depth of your emotions and paves the way for closure. Seeking closure can be a personal journey, where individuals explore various avenues to find peace. Some may turn to dialogue and communication with those involved, while others might prefer introspection or even rituals that symbolize releasing the hurt. The process of finding closure varies significantly among people; all methods aim to bring inner tranquility and dissolve lingering resentment (JONES, 2024).

In exploring how to forgive and seek closure, it's helpful to consider practical steps or guidelines. First, it's crucial to allow yourself time. Forgiveness doesn't happen overnight; it's a gradual process of coming to terms with what has occurred and deciding to move forward. Writing about the experience, talking to trusted friends or professionals, or practicing mindfulness can facilitate this process. Each method allows for self-exploration and ultimately helps lay a foundation for genuine forgiveness.

Importantly, as you work through the process of letting go, remember that forgiveness is not just about the person who wronged you. It's about freeing yourself from the emotional entanglements that hold you back. By releasing these negative emotions, you contribute directly to your own well-being and alter the dynamics of your relationships positively. When you let go of grudges, you make room for healing and growth, leading to more fulfilling interactions with others. This shift can enhance communication, foster understanding, and build a stronger, more resilient bond between people (JONES, 2024).

Moreover, the act of letting go benefits not only personal well-being but also relationship dynamics. Holding onto anger can perpetually strain relationships, making it difficult to establish trust and open communication. By choosing to forgive, you effectively change the narrative of your interactions. You become more empathetic and understanding, which encourages others to mirror these sentiments. In this way, forgiveness acts as a catalyst, transforming strained connections into supportive and nurturing ones.

This transformation can be particularly significant in close relationships, such as those with family and friends, where deep ties create complex emotional landscapes. In these contexts, forgiveness underpins a supportive atmosphere that is conducive to open dialogue and mutual respect. Recognizing when misunderstandings occur and addressing them with a forgiving mindset can prevent long-term rifts and cultivate lasting harmony.

To illustrate further, consider how forgiveness impacts day-to-day interactions. A young professional who practices forgiveness might find they are less likely to react defensively to workplace challenges, thereby promoting a more cooperative and productive environment. Similarly, college students who embrace forgiveness can enjoy better mental health, resulting in more stable friendships and study groups. This positive outlook and reduced stress can contribute significantly to their academic and social success.

It's important to remember, however, that forgiveness is a personal journey unique to each individual. While some might find it easier, others may need support and guidance. Being patient with oneself and seeking help if needed can ensure the journey towards forgiveness is both effective and empowering (How Forgiveness Is Imperative to Deep Emotional Healing + 4 Healing Forgiveness Affirmations, 2018).

Final Thoughts

In this chapter, we've delved into the ways you can nurture connections with friends and family through intentional actions. By scheduling regular quality time and engaging in shared activities, we create opportunities to bond more deeply. These moments go beyond just having fun; they cushion our lives with comfort, shared stories, and mutual understanding. Amidst life's busyness, making the effort for meaningful interaction helps reveal the people behind their daily roles, fostering genuine communication and trust. It's these deliberate acts of connection that provide a sense of belonging and security amid life's uncertainties.

The key is finding a balance between quality and quantity of time spent together, emphasizing meaningful engagement over rushed hours. Respect and attention during these times not only cultivate appreciation but also strengthen the bonds we share, ensuring they're enduring and supportive. By embracing such practices, you enrich your relationships, setting the foundation for emotional well-being across both personal and professional spheres. These connections become a crucial support system, echoing the resilience needed as you navigate through the complexities of adulthood while encouraging emotional growth and happiness.

11

Embracing Empathy

Develop an Empathetic Mindset to Enhance Interpersonal Relationships

Developing an empathetic mindset is a key aspect of building meaningful and deep interpersonal relationships. Empathy allows us to connect with others on a level that transcends mere words, enabling us to understand their emotions and experiences more profoundly. When we genuinely empathize with someone, we are not just hearing them; we are truly listening and feeling alongside them. This chapter will explore how embracing empathy can transform the quality of our connections, making them more authentic and satisfying.

Throughout the chapter, we'll delve into practical strategies for cultivating empathy in everyday interactions. You'll learn how becoming an active observer can help you tune into non-verbal cues, gaining insights beyond what is spoken. The chapter also highlights the importance of deep listening, encouraging you to be present without the urge to immediately respond. By asking thoughtful questions and engaging in perspective-taking exercises, you'll discover new ways to bridge emotional gaps between you and others. Ultimately, this journey towards empathy not only enhances your interpersonal skills but also fosters a more supportive and understanding environment in both personal and professional settings.

Recognize the Feelings and Perspectives of Others

Understanding the emotions and viewpoints of others is a fundamental aspect of cultivating empathy and creating strong interpersonal connections. Empathy allows us to step into another person's shoes, to truly understand their experiences and feelings, which ultimately leads to more fulfilling and authentic relationships. To foster this empathetic mindset, it's important to delve deeper into the techniques that can enhance our ability to connect with others on an emotional level.

One effective method to develop empathy is to become an active observer, which involves keenly noticing non-verbal cues such as body language. Non-verbal communication often speaks louder than words. For instance, a friend's crossed arms and downcast eyes might indicate discomfort or sadness, even if they verbally claim to be fine. Recognizing these unspoken signals requires conscious effort and practice. By focusing on gestures, facial expressions, and posture, we can gain valuable insights into what someone might be feeling beneath their surface words (Reid, 2022).

Deep listening plays a pivotal role in validating others' feelings and fostering meaningful dialogue. Unlike standard listening, deep listening demands full attention, free from interruptions or the urge to immediately respond. It means being fully present in the moment and absorbing not only the words but also the emotions conveyed. When we listen intently, we create a safe space for others to express themselves, and this validation can deepen our connection. For example, during a conversation, rather than thinking about your response or interrupting, simply nodding affirmatively and maintaining eye contact encourages the speaker to continue sharing, knowing they are truly heard (Lesley University, 2019).

Asking thoughtful questions further enhances emotional exchanges and clears up potential misunderstandings. Open-ended questions, such as "How did you feel about that situation?" or "What do you think might have caused this?" prompt the other person to explore their emotions and thoughts more deeply. These inquiries not only show your interest in understanding them better but also help clarify any unclear aspects of their story. Thoughtful questioning invites individuals to share more openly and reflectively, which enriches the dialogue and strengthens the emotional bond between you.

Moreover, practicing perspective-taking is essential for empathizing with others and building emotional connections. Perspective-taking involves imagining what it must be like to live in someone else's world, complete with their unique challenges, triumphs, and feelings. This mental exercise can help bridge emotional gaps and dissolve barriers created by differing experiences or backgrounds. For example, if a colleague seems unusually stressed about meeting a deadline, trying to visualize the pressures they face at work and home could lead to a deeper understanding and a more supportive interaction. Studies suggest that engaging in perspective-taking activities regularly can significantly boost one's capacity for empathy, ultimately nurturing healthier relationships (Reid, 2022).

Guidance on effectively becoming an active observer, listener, questioner, and perspective-taker can transform how we interact with others. Active observation starts with small changes, like consciously observing people in everyday settings without jumping to conclusions. Note the subtleties—gestures, expressions, and tones—that tell stories beyond spoken words. Similarly, deep listening requires practice in resisting distractions, such as constantly checking your phone or letting your mind wander during conversations. Setting aside dedicated time to practice focused listening in each interaction gradually reinforces this skill.

Incorporating thoughtful questioning into dialogues doesn't mean interrogating the other person relentlessly, but rather embedding naturally curious questions into the conversation flow. Questions should aim to uncover deeper layers rather than satisfy superficial curiosity. Practicing asking open-ended questions and then patiently hearing out the respondent's full answer helps hone this approach.

Lastly, perspective-taking can be cultivated through imaginative exercises. Challenge yourself to actively consider scenarios from others' viewpoints, seeking to understand their journey and emotional landscape. Role-playing exercises or reading diverse narratives can widen your empathetic scope, making it easier to relate to various perspectives in real-life interactions.

Differentiate Between Sympathy and Empathy

Understanding the distinction between sympathy and empathy is vital for developing more constructive interpersonal engagements. While these terms are often used interchangeably, they represent different attitudes and approaches to human interaction. Sympathy involves feeling pity or sorrow for someone else's situation without necessarily understanding their feelings. In contrast, empathy means feeling with someone, seeing the world from their perspective, and sharing in their emotional experiences.

When we clearly distinguish between feeling for someone (sympathy) and feeling with someone (empathy), we enhance our relational bonds. Sympathy creates a separation between individuals; it maintains a distance because it does not engage with the emotional depth of another person's experience. For instance, sending a sympathy card when someone faces a loss acknowledges the event but keeps interactions formal. This gesture demonstrates caring but lacks the deeper connection needed for strong relationships, especially when the individual involved desires support. It's like observing someone's life from the outside rather than participating in it. Conversely, empathy demands that we step into the shoes of others. It involves understanding how they feel by actively listening and connecting to their emotions, fostering genuine closeness.

Identifying the emotional responses tied to each approach helps us see why empathy fosters closeness and understanding, while sympathy might inadvertently create distance. Emotional responses in empathetic interactions are characterized by a mutual vulnerability and shared understanding. When you express empathy, you acknowledge the other person's emotional state and show them they are not alone in their struggles. This response builds trust and makes the other person feel understood and valued. On the other hand, sympathy can sometimes lead to unintentional judgment or the need to offer solutions, which might make the person in distress feel misunderstood or devalued. They may perceive an attitude of superiority, where sympathizers unknowingly convey relief at not being in the same situation, thus creating emotional space.

Examining how sympathy and empathy manifest in communication further illustrates these differences. Communication rooted in empathy is about listening more than speaking, allowing the person facing hardship to express themselves openly. Empathetic communication invites dialogue where both parties share experiences and emotions equitably. For example, when a friend shares their personal struggle, instead of giving unsolicited advice or saying, "I'm sorry you're going through this," an empathic response would be, "I'm here for you if you want to talk." This approach transitions from offering pity to sharing genuine experiences. It encourages openness and honesty, where both individuals willingly participate in the exchange of emotions.

Furthermore, empathetic responses contribute significantly to greater trust and relational satisfaction. Trust is built on the foundation of understanding and respect, which empathy naturally provides. It reassures people that their feelings are valid and safe to express. This safety leads to stronger bonds and increases the satisfaction one gets from their relationships. Consider a scenario in the workplace where a colleague feels overwhelmed by their workload. While sympathetic colleagues might say, "That must be tough," empathetic ones could go the extra mile by recognizing the stress and asking how they can assist, which strengthens teamwork and collaboration. By doing so, they transform the work environment into a space where employees feel supported and included, improving overall morale.

Empathy requires effort and the willingness to open oneself up to another's vulnerabilities. It is not always easy, especially in situations that don't directly affect you. However, the practice of empathy enriches interpersonal relationships by fostering deeper connections and mutual respect. The ability to listen without judgment, understand without agreeing, and provide support without advice comes from an empathic mindset, which enhances the quality of our interactions.

Tailor Your Responses to Show Genuine Understanding

Crafting responses that reflect genuine understanding plays a crucial role in enhancing the quality of our interactions. Empathy is not just about feeling for someone else but truly comprehending their perspective and emotions. At the heart of this is reflective listening, a skill that can transform how we communicate. Reflective listening involves paraphrasing or restating what the other person has expressed to confirm your understanding and reassure them that they've been heard.

Reflective listening might seem straightforward, yet it requires mindfulness and practice. When you listen to someone, try to grasp not only the words they are saying but also the emotions and intent behind them. For instance, if a friend says, "I'm really stressed about work," you might respond with, "It sounds like you're overwhelmed with everything going on." This type of response shows that you've captured the essence of their message while providing them reassurance that their concerns matter. By doing so, you help create an environment where the speaker feels safe to express themselves further without fear of being misunderstood or judged.

Another powerful aspect of empathetic communication is personalizing interactions by sharing personal experiences. Doing so can significantly deepen bonds as it builds common ground between individuals. However, it's crucial to balance sharing without overshadowing the speaker's experience. Imagine a colleague confides about a difficult project. Instead of merely talking about your own struggles with similar projects, you could say, "I remember facing something challenging too, and here's what helped me. But I'm here to support you however I can." This approach acknowledges their situation and offers solidarity without shifting the focus away from them.

Tone and language hold immense potential in nurturing a space conducive to openness. The way we phrase our responses and the tone we use can either build bridges or erect barriers. Gentle, thoughtful language promotes trust and encourages sharing. Suppose you're in a conversation where emotions are high; maintaining a calm and warm tone can defuse tension and ensure clarity prevails. Additionally, simple affirmations like "I understand" or "That makes sense" can convey empathy and acceptance.

Validating emotions is another cornerstone of empathetic interactions. Recognizing and affirming someone's feelings validates their experiences, empowering them to open up more freely. Validation doesn't necessarily mean you agree with how someone feels, but it shows you accept their emotional state as legitimate. For instance, if a friend expresses sadness over a setback and worries they're being silly, a validating response might be, "Your feelings are understandable; it was meaningful to you." Such reassurances can significantly uplift others, reinforcing that their emotions are acceptable and worthy of attention.

Incorporating reflective listening, personalization, attention to tone, and emotional validation in our daily conversations requires intention and patience. As young adults, college students, and professionals navigating various relationships, these skills can help forge deeper connections at school, work, or home. A practical step is to practice active listening—focusing wholly on the speaker without distractions. Eliminating interruptions, such as electronic devices, can signal your full engagement and respect.

Remember, effective communication isn't about having all the right answers but about being present and engaged. Maintaining eye contact, using positive body language, and nodding while someone speaks can reinforce that you're invested in the exchange. When you actively validate their feelings, you pave the way for more open dialogues and mutual understanding.

Ultimately, developing an empathetic mindset takes time, practice, and continuous learning. These skills aren't only valuable in personal settings but are also instrumental in professional environments. Practicing empathy in workplace discussions, performance reviews, and team projects can lead to better collaboration, creative problem-solving, and conflict resolution.

Avoid Judgment and Foster Open-Mindedness

Practicing non-reactivity is an essential step in creating an open environment for dialogue, allowing individuals to express sensitive topics without fear of judgment or reprisal. It involves exercising patience and emotional integrity, which encourages open communication and deeper connections. When you practice non-reactivity, you're essentially hitting the pause button on your immediate responses, especially those driven by strong emotions or preconceived notions. This approach fosters a calm space for critical conversations, where everyone feels heard and valued.

Imagine this scenario: you're in a heated discussion with a colleague about a work project. The natural instinct might be to interrupt or rebut their points before they finish speaking. However, if you consciously decide to remain silent, absorb what's being said, and respond thoughtfully rather than re-actively, the conversation becomes less about winning an argument and more about finding a solution together. This practice not only enhances understanding but also paves the way for collaboration, reinforcing a sense of trust and respect within the relationship (Rcademy, 2023).

Cultivating curiosity is another cornerstone in fostering empathy and building stronger interpersonal relationships. When we explore the reasons behind others' emotions, we gain insights into their worldviews and experiences. This curiosity should be genuine and free from any judgment. It's not about satisfying our own need for information but about understanding the depths of someone else's emotional landscape.

For instance, if a friend confides in you about a personal

struggle, show interest by asking open-ended questions that invite them to elaborate further. Instead of immediately offering advice or sharing your own experiences, encourage them to share more about their feelings and thoughts. Questions like "What makes you feel this way?" or "Can you tell me more about what you're experiencing?" help in digging deeper into their narrative. This kind of engagement not only validates their experience but also builds a bridge of empathy between you, as it shows you genuinely care about understanding their situation from their perspective (RCADEMY, 2023).

Addressing and challenging stereotypes is crucial for personal growth and empathy development. Stereotypes often stem from ingrained societal biases that lead to oversimplified and inaccurate perceptions of people based on race, gender, age, or other characteristics. These generalizations can severely hinder our ability to empathize with others by clouding our judgment.

To counteract this, we should consistently reflect on and question our biases. Engaging in self-reflection allows us to identify these internalized stereotypes and actively work against them. Imagine interacting with someone from a cultural background different from your own. Instead of relying on preconceived notions you've heard through media or secondhand stories, take the initiative to understand their individual experiences. Ask yourself if your assumptions are based on stereotypes, and strive to replace them with factual, firsthand interactions and knowledge. This conscious effort not only broadens our perspectives but also deepens our empathy towards diverse groups.

Embracing diversity in perspectives and experiences is the final piece in promoting a non-judgmental attitude within interpersonal relationships. When we open ourselves to various viewpoints, we enrich our understanding and grow both personally and socially. Each person's unique life experiences contribute valuable insights, adding layers to our collective human experience.

Consider engaging with people from different backgrounds, cultures, or professions in your daily life. Attend cultural festivals, join diverse community groups, or simply have conversations with colleagues who have distinct viewpoints. These experiences challenge our existing beliefs and push us to consider alternate ways of thinking. By welcoming this diversity, we create spaces where differences are celebrated rather than tolerated. The result is a more inclusive society where personal growth and collective empathy are ongoing processes.

Bringing It All Together

Understanding and applying empathy doesn't just change how we see others—it transforms how we connect with them. This chapter dives into the essence of empathy, highlighting that it's more than just feeling for someone but truly putting ourselves in their shoes to appreciate their experiences and emotions. By recognizing non-verbal signals and engaging in deep listening, we unlock a new way of interaction where words are not the only means of communication. Asking thoughtful questions and practicing perspective-taking allows us to see the world as others do, nurturing relationships built on understanding and closeness. As we differentiate between empathy and sympathy, it becomes clear that empathy strengthens bonds by making others feel genuinely heard and valued.

To tailor our responses for genuine understanding, reflective listening is crucial. It's about showing we're present and invested through our reactions and tone. Sharing personal experiences thoughtfully can deepen connections without overshadowing others' stories. Moreover, avoiding judgment helps us foster an open-minded space for dialogue, paving the way for honest exchanges rich with mutual respect. Embracing diverse perspectives challenges stereotypes and broadens our worldview, encouraging growth and empathy. Throughout this journey, cultivating empathy requires effort and patience, but its impact is profound—transforming not only individual relationships but also the spaces we inhabit, be it at home, college, or work.

12

Balancing Work and Self-Care

Achieving Career and Well-being Harmony

Achieving a harmonious blend between career aspirations and personal well-being is more than a balancing act—it's an art. In the fast-paced environment of today's world, finding this equilibrium can seem elusive, yet it remains a vital pursuit for anyone looking to thrive both professionally and personally. As young adults, college students, or budding professionals, we often juggle numerous responsibilities while striving to meet our own goals and maintain happiness. The key lies in understanding how to align our ambitions with practical expectations, thus avoiding the pitfalls of burnout that come from overreaching. Recognizing individual capacity becomes foundational, much like establishing a strong base for a structure destined to withstand time and pressure.

This chapter will guide you through setting realistic career objectives while emphasizing well-being. It introduces the

SMART criteria to ensure your goals are not only ambitious but also grounded in reality. We'll explore time management techniques designed to enhance productivity without sacrificing mental health, showing how strategies like the Pomodoro Technique or time blocking can optimize both effort and results. Additionally, we'll delve into the importance of flexibility and regular reassessment of goals to adapt as life's circumstances change. By integrating these methodologies, you'll discover how to merge career advancement with personal growth, ensuring that neither is neglected in the pursuit of success. Join us as we navigate the intersection of professional drive and life satisfaction, revealing how the two can coexist harmoniously when approached thoughtfully.

Set Realistic Career Expectations and Timelines

Achieving a harmonious blend of career aspirations and personal well-being requires a deep understanding of one's unique capabilities. Recognizing your capacity is the cornerstone in setting achievable goals, vital for avoiding the dreaded burnout that can happen when ambition overshadows reality. Regardless of how grand our dreams might be, aligning them with a realistic assessment of what we can manage effectively is crucial. Consider this as establishing a foundation for constructing a building. Without a sturdy base, no structure can stand tall. Similarly, acknowledging personal limits helps in creating robust, yet attainable goals, serving as a preventative measure against the frustration that comes with unmet expectations.

To maintain focus and feasibility in goal-setting, adopting the SMART criteria—Specific, Measurable, Achievable, Relevant, and Time-bound—is recommended. This structured approach helps break down ambitions into manageable components. For instance, instead of aspiring to 'improve work performance,' one might set the specific goal of 'completing an online course related to job responsibilities within three months.' This specificity not only clarifies the path forward but also provides tangible milestones that keep motivation high. The measurable aspect adds an element of accountability, ensuring progress is not just hopeful but visible and definitive (*SMART Goals to Improve Your Time Management Skills*, n.d.).

The achievability and relevance components serve as a reality check. It's essential to question whether the goal fits within current resource availability, skills, and time constraints. Ambition without practicality can lead to disillusionment. Therefore, determining if a goal is realistically attainable is akin to deciding if you have all the necessary ingredients before starting a recipe. Relevance ensures alignment with broader life objectives, reinforcing the idea that goals should contribute meaningfully to overall aspirations (*SMART Goals to Improve Your Time Management Skills*, n.d.).

Time management techniques like the Pomodoro Technique or time blocking offer invaluable support in increasing productivity and maintainability of tasks. These strategies split tasks into focused intervals, often with short breaks, enhancing concentration and preventing mental fatigue. Picture yourself working intensely for 25 minutes on a task, followed by a five-minute break. This rhythm keeps the brain fresh and reduces procrastination odds. Alternately, time blocking involves allocating specific time slots to different tasks throughout the day. By scheduling particular hours for distinct activities, you create a daily routine that maximizes efficiency and minimizes distractions. This approach, much like having a detailed travel itinerary, assures you're utilizing every minute wisely, eliminating the chaos of overlapping priorities.

Regularly reassessing goals offers a dynamic element to planning and adaptation, recognizing that life's circumstances are rarely static. Continuous reflection allows for the adjustment of goals to ensure they remain relevant and aligned with changing priorities and resources (*SMART Goals to Improve Your Time Management Skills*, n.d.). Think of it as navigating a ship across the sea; changing winds necessitate course adjustments to reach the intended destination. This adaptability not only preserves engagement and motivation but also cultivates self-awareness, empowering you to make informed decisions about future endeavors.

Implementing these strategies within the scope of young adults, college students, and young professionals serves as a powerful tool to balance the demands of transitioning into adulthood. Young adults grappling with new-found independence and responsibility benefit from recognizing their personal capacity, thus setting realistic expectations across school, work, and relationships. Aligning their aspirations with practical outcomes minimizes stress and enhances fulfillment.

College students, often overwhelmed by academic obligations, social life, and the quest for emotional stability, find solace in SMART goal-setting. It promotes efficient study habits, prioritizes coursework deadlines, and structures time effectively around social engagements. As students assess their goals regularly, they're better equipped to adapt to shifts in academic pressure and personal growth, nurturing a balanced lifestyle that supports mental well-being.

For young professionals striving to excel in their careers while maintaining meaningful personal connections, the blend of recognized capacity and SMART criteria is instrumental. It aids in setting achievable career milestones without sacrificing health or happiness. Techniques like time-blocking help manage workplace demands and personal endeavors, nurturing an environment where professional success does not come at the expense of personal joy.

Schedule Self-Care Activities Just Like Meetings

In today's hectic world, achieving a balance between career goals and personal well-being can seem like a daunting task. However, one crucial step in reaching this harmony is prioritizing self-care as a fundamental part of your daily schedule, just as important as any work commitment. Realizing the significance of self-care means recognizing that taking time for yourself isn't an indulgence; it's a necessity. Incorporating self-care into your routine requires deliberate planning and steadfast adherence to ensure your overall well-being doesn't fall by the wayside.

First and foremost, allocating specific times for breaks throughout your day isn't just beneficial—it's essential. Regular breaks have been shown to improve mental health and boost productivity, leading to more efficient work sessions. By stepping away from your tasks periodically, you allow your mind to rejuvenate, resulting in clearer thinking and better performance once you return. Without these moments of rest, stress accumulates, eventually leading to burnout or decreased productivity. Taking short, frequent breaks— whether it's a five-minute stretch every hour or a dedicated hour for lunch without distractions—can make a world of difference in maintaining your mental health and enhancing your work output.

Integrating self-care activities into your calendar is another effective strategy for ensuring consistency and commitment to your well-being practices. Just as meetings and deadlines are non-negotiable, setting aside time specifically for self-care should be considered equally critical. By physically scheduling these activities, you create a tangible reminder of their importance, which helps reinforce the habit over time. Whether it's blocking out time for a walk, scheduling a yoga session, or simply having 30 minutes to read a book, having it marked on your calendar signals its priority. This consistent practice not only reinforces the value of self-care in your life but also ensures that it remains a regular part of your routine amidst other obligations.

However, while consistency is key, it's also vital to maintain some flexibility in how you approach self-care scheduling. Life is unpredictable, and rigid routines can sometimes add unnecessary stress rather than alleviate it. Allowing for adaptability in your self-care approach fosters realistic practices that can accommodate varying demands and unforeseen events. For instance, if a work deadline prevents you from following your usual self-care routine, being flexible enough to adjust your plans instead of skipping them altogether can help maintain your well-being. Perhaps an evening meditation session or a quick workout can replace your afternoon walk, ensuring you still attend to your personal needs without feeling guilty or frazzled.

Moreover, engaging in a diverse range of self-care activities supports holistic well-being. Self-care isn't one-size-fits-all;

what works for one person might not benefit another in the same way. Exploring different activities allows you to discover what truly resonates with you, promoting physical, mental, and emotional health. For instance, while some may find solace in physical exercise, others might gravitate towards creative pursuits such as painting or writing, which offer an outlet for expression and relaxation. Involving yourself in varied activities—from mindfulness practices to social interactions with friends—not only provides comprehensive benefits but also keeps self-care interesting and fulfilling, reducing any sense of monotony.

Crucially, it's important to overcome common obstacles that may arise when prioritizing self-care. One significant challenge is dealing with feelings of guilt for taking time away from responsibilities. Many people struggle with the belief that focusing on themselves detracts from their ability to fulfill other duties. Yet, as emphasized by experts, self-care is a necessary investment in long-term effectiveness and satisfaction. Thus, normalizing the need for breaks and communicating boundaries to those around you helps mitigate guilt and encourages others to respect your self-care time. Expressing these boundaries clearly also alleviates interruptions, allowing you to enjoy your self-care activities fully and reap their benefits.

By reflecting on the advantages of self-care, such as increased energy and improved mood, you can further motivate yourself to prioritize it regularly. The positive outcomes of self-care ultimately enhance relationships, work performance, and overall happiness, reinforcing its indispensable role in our lives. It's crucial to remember that valuing self-care doesn't mean neglecting other responsibilities; instead, it positions you to perform better across all areas.

Utilize Deep Work Techniques for Productivity

In today's fast-paced world, achieving a balance between career aspirations and well-being can often feel like an uphill battle. One powerful approach to managing this challenge is by integrating deep work methods into our daily routines. Deep work focuses on engaging in professional activities performed in a state of distraction-free concentration, pushing cognitive limits, and ultimately enhancing focus and effectiveness in one's workload (Deep Work: How To Kill Distractions And Boost Productivity, 2021).

Understanding the essence of deep work is crucial. In an era where distractions are plentiful and constant, it becomes increasingly difficult to produce quality outcomes. Yet, by embracing deep work principles, individuals can drastically increase the quality of their output while minimizing the interference from everyday disruptions. The majority of professionals unknowingly engage in what Cal Newport describes as shallow work—tasks that demand minimal cognitive effort and are often executed amid diversions (Asana, n.d.). By contrast, dedicating time to deep work not only refines one's skills but also imparts a sense of mastery and fulfillment which is often missing in the hurried pace of modern life.

Creating a workspace that minimizes distractions is equally significant. Our environment plays a substantial role in our ability to concentrate and stay motivated. A cluttered or noisy workspace can lead to fragmented attention and decreased motivation. Hence, organizing your physical and digital spaces to eliminate unnecessary distractions fosters an ambiance conducive to deep concentration. This could involve turning off notifications on your devices, arranging a comfortable and organized desk, or even using noise-cancelling headphones during work sessions. Such adjustments create a dedicated space where focus can thrive, making it easier to delve deeply into challenging tasks without the risk of being derailed by external interruptions.

A critical component of deep work is the strategic scheduling of uninterrupted time blocks. Allocating specific periods solely for deep work can support single-tasking and significantly boost accomplishment rates. For example, many individuals find that setting aside the morning hours for intensive work allows them to capitalize on peak mental performance. Blocking out these times in personal calendars, alongside enabling features such as 'Do Not Disturb' modes on devices, can distribute your attention exclusively towards tasks requiring undivided focus. Integrating rituals or routines that signal the start of deep work sessions can further reinforce this practice. Over time, this habit-forming approach nurtures a reliable method to achieve consistency in productivity.

As you engage in these periods of concentrated effort, regularly evaluating progress is advisable. Reflecting on what worked and what didn't in past sessions provides invaluable insights. It guides necessary adjustments in one's productivity strategies. For instance, if distractions still seep through despite existing measures, identifying the triggers can help tailor more effective solutions. Moreover, tracking progress allows individuals to acknowledge growth, reinforcing the positive impact that deep work has had on both personal capabilities and professional achievements. Keeping a journal or using apps designed to monitor tasks can assist in analyzing how effectively time is utilized and highlight areas needing improvement.

Identify Burnout Early and Counteract It

Understanding and managing burnout is crucial in today's fast-paced world, especially for young adults who balance career aspirations with personal well-being. Recognizing early signs of burnout can empower individuals to act preemptively, preventing further stress from manifesting into significant health issues.

To start, identifying burnout symptoms is essential for proactive stress management. Burnout doesn't happen overnight; it creeps in as we push ourselves beyond reasonable limits. Common signs include chronic exhaustion, heightened irritability, and a sense of detachment from work or personal relationships. These symptoms can interfere with daily life, making routine tasks feel overwhelming (Fraga, 2018). Recognizing these signs early can be a game-changer, enabling you to take preventive measures before reaching a breaking point.

One such measure is incorporating structured recovery periods into your daily routine, forming the backbone of a burnout prevention plan. Regular breaks are not just about resting but are pivotal in building resilience against stress. For instance, scheduling short intervals throughout the day to step away from work can recharge your mental batteries and enhance focus when you return to tasks. Think of these breaks as opportunities to refresh your energy, similar to charging a smartphone battery. This practice helps maintain a steady state of well-being, ensuring that you don't deplete your resources too quickly.

In addition to breaks, seeking support through open communication is vital in alleviating feelings of isolation that often accompany stress. Emotional support from friends, family, or colleagues can offer a different perspective on challenging situations, reducing feelings of being overwhelmed (Smith & Reid, 2018). Having someone to share your thoughts with can lighten emotional burdens and provide reassurance that you're not alone in your struggles. Remember, asking for help is not a sign of weakness; rather, it's an indication of self-awareness and willingness to manage stress effectively.

Regular reflection practices also serve as critical barometers for managing workloads and understanding your emotional state. Reflection doesn't need to be complicated. It can include journaling thoughts at the end of each day, meditating, or taking a quiet walk to clear your mind. When you reflect, you gain insights into how certain activities affect your mood and energy levels. This awareness helps in adjusting your schedule or tasks according to what works best for your mental health. Reflection acts like a mirror, showing you where adjustments are needed to maintain balance and prevent burnout.

The key to achieving harmony between career ambitions and well-being lies in the consistent application of these strategies. Revisiting your goals regularly can ensure they align with your current capabilities and needs, allowing you to adapt more readily to new challenges. This adaptability is crucial because life is dynamic, and learning to flow with changes prevents rigid patterns that often lead to burnout (Fraga, 2018).

Moreover, creating a supportive environment both at home and at work can foster an atmosphere conducive to mental wellness. Sharing responsibilities, whether at work with teammates or at home with family, reduces the burden on a single individual, promoting collaboration and collective problem-solving. This collaborative approach enhances over-all morale and creates a network of mutual support, essential for maintaining a healthy balance.

Bringing It All Together

As we wrap up the chapter, it's evident that finding a balance between career goals and personal well-being is both an art and a science. We've explored the importance of setting realistic expectations and timelines to avoid burnout. By acknowledging our unique capabilities, we can align our ambitions with what we can realistically achieve, much like laying a strong founda-tion for a building. Embracing the SMART criteria allows us to break down big dreams into manageable steps, ensuring that each goal is specific and attainable. This clarity not only keeps motivation high but also prevents frustration when our lofty aspirations don't immediately materialize. For young adults, college students, and budding professionals, this approach offers guidance as they juggle school, work, and relationships in the dynamic journey toward adulthood.

Moreover, fostering productivity through deep work tech-niques and scheduling self-care as non-negotiable aspects of daily life are highlighted as essential strategies. Implementing focused work sessions enhances concentration and effective-ness, while also offering moments to step back and recharge. Regularly reassessing our goals amid changing circumstances ensures they remain relevant, much like adjusting a ship's course to navigate turbulent waters. Alongside these strategies, prioritizing diverse self-care activities reinforces the impor-tance of nurturing mental health. In acknowledging the signs of burnout early, we gain the power to counteract stress before it escalates. Remember, the road to success shouldn't come at the expense of well-being; instead, it's about harmoniously blending our professional and personal lives to flourish in all areas.

13

Harnessing the Power of Reflection

Utilize Reflective Practices to Gain Insights into Your Personal Growth

Reflective practices are an essential approach to personal growth and self-awareness, offering tools to explore our inner worlds and understand our journey. As we traverse the path of adulthood with its myriad challenges—be it academic pressure, workplace stress, or relationship juggling—it's easy to feel lost amidst the chaos. Reflective practices provide a moment of pause, allowing us to step back and assess where we stand. These practices aren't just for dwelling on what's past but involve actively engaging with our experiences to gain insights that propel us forward. They encourage a deep dive into understanding ourselves better, enhancing emotional intelligence, and fostering a richer appreciation of our personal narratives.

In this chapter, we're going to explore various methods of using reflective practices to boost self-awareness and aid in personal development. We'll delve into the art of journaling as a powerful tool for organizing thoughts and emotions, creating a space for goal setting, and maintaining consistent focus and accountability. The journey will guide you through utilizing prompts for introspective thinking, encouraging exploration beyond daily events to uncover meaningful insights about life experiences. We'll also examine how creating a feedback loop by reviewing past entries can highlight personal growth, allowing young professionals or students to recognize shifts in their long-term trajectories. This chapter is designed to equip you with the practical strategies and reflective techniques necessary to harness the power of self-reflection for personal evolution, ensuring that every step you take is both informed and intentional.

Keep a Journal to Track Personal Evolution

Journaling is often seen as a simple activity, but it has the profound potential to serve as a powerful tool for self-discovery. The act of journaling offers therapeutic benefits by providing an outlet for emotional release and helping to organize thoughts, which leads to enhanced clarity. When individuals engage in writing down their feelings and experiences, they unlock a path to better understand themselves and their emotions. This process of externalizing internal dialogue can be incredibly liberating, allowing one to see their thoughts from a new perspective. This technique can aid young adults, college students, and young professionals who face stressful situations, like navigating academic pressures or workplace challenges.

One of the key elements that make journaling effective is its ability to set specific goals. In the hustle and bustle of adulthood, focusing on personal aspirations can become overshadowed by immediate concerns. By articulating goals in a journal, individuals create a roadmap for self-improvement. Writing these goals helps maintain consistent focus and accountability. For instance, a college student might outline academic achievements they aim to reach each semester, while a young professional could note career milestones or personal development targets. The act of writing instills a sense of commitment, making it easier to track progress and provide motivation during times of uncertainty or frustration.

Utilizing prompts is another way journaling can deepen self-reflection. Prompts guide the writer toward introspective thinking and uncover meaningful insights about life experiences. These prompts might ask questions like "What were my biggest challenges this week and how did I handle them?" or "Describe a moment today where I felt most myself." Such queries encourage young adults to delve into their personal narratives, exploring not just daily events but also their reactions and feelings about those events. By engaging with these prompts regularly, individuals gain a richer understanding of their identity and values—insights that are crucial when facing life's transitions.

Creating a feedback loop through reviewing past entries is an invaluable part of journaling. This practice not only informs future actions but also highlights personal growth over time. By looking back at what was written weeks, months, or even years ago, writers can see patterns in their thoughts and behaviors. This reflection helps identify areas of progress and makes it easier to replicate positive outcomes in the future. It's particularly beneficial for young professionals to recognize how they've evolved in their careers or managed complex projects. Meanwhile, for students, it's a chance to see shifts in their academic journey and social dynamics over successive semesters.

For many, journaling becomes more than just a sporadic activity; it's a habit that evolves alongside its practitioner. With consistency, a journal transforms into a historical record of one's personal journey, encapsulating triumphs and tribulations alike. Engaging deeply with this reflective practice empowers individuals to reassess previous decisions critically yet compassionately, enhancing their decision-making skills and emotional resilience.

Incorporating guidelines within journaling practices can elevate them further. When setting specific goals, it is helpful to categorize them, perhaps dividing goals into short-term, such as completing a certain amount of reading per day, and long-term, like writing a thesis paper by the semester's end. By breaking down larger goals into smaller steps, each achievement feels more attainable. Similarly, using prompts effectively might involve selecting themes related to current life challenges, such as work-life balance or relationship dynamics, tailored to reflect ongoing struggles and triumphs.

Moreover, creating a feedback loop can be structured by dedicating time each month to review and reflect on past entries intentionally. Setting aside moments for this kind of contemplation fosters a deeper recognition of growth and changes in mindset. The continuity offered by reviewing old journal entries encourages young adults to honor both minor victories and significant breakthroughs, reinforcing self-awareness and confidence.

Engage in Periodic Life Audits to Evaluate Direction

Life audits are a vital tool for young adults, college students, and young professionals trying to navigate adulthood's challenges. Conducting regular life audits enables an intentional examination of one's current life situation. It encourages introspection on personal and professional goals, helping you assess how aligned your daily actions are with your desired direction in life. A life audit allows you to step back from the chaos and noise of everyday routines and focus on what truly matters.

By setting aside time for self-reflection, individuals can uncover their true values and desires. Life audits push you to look beyond superficial achievements and dig deeper into what brings genuine satisfaction and happiness. This process is essential as it helps identify whether the choices made currently align with long-term aspirations. The insights gained from this can be transformative, allowing you to shape a future that resonates with both personal and professional objectives.

Conducting a life audit involves evaluating key areas such as career, relationships, health, and personal development. For instance, examining your career trajectory might reveal a mismatch between your current job and your passion, urging a reevaluation of professional paths or skills needed for advancement. Similarly, assessing relationships can highlight connections that either empower or drain you, leading to more intentional interactions. Meanwhile, reflecting on your health and personal development can unearth habits that need modification for improved well-being and fulfillment.

Understanding these facets of life through an audit provides clarity and perspective, making it easier to prioritize tasks that contribute to overall happiness and success. By doing so, you create a roadmap to focus efforts on what genuinely deserves attention. It's crucial to approach this evaluation process with honesty and self-compassion, recognizing that acknowledging areas needing improvement is a sign of strength, not weakness.

Post-audit, crafting an action plan with SMART (Specific, Measurable, Achievable, Relevant, Time-bound) goals is necessary to address the findings. Establishing clear, actionable steps based on audit outcomes enhances the potential for achieving goals. Whether it's changing a career path, nurturing meaningful relationships, or improving health, a strategic plan propels you toward tangible results. For example, if the audit reveals a desire to improve physical health, set specific fitness goals like running a 5k in six months or incorporating a balanced diet plan.

Moreover, life audits encourage flexibility in adapting strategies according to the outcomes. Change should not be feared but embraced as a sign of growth. As your personal and professional landscapes shift, being open to adjusting plans ensures continued alignment with evolving goals. For instance, if an opportunity arises that was unforeseen during the initial audit, adapt your strategy to incorporate this new development, keeping your objectives dynamic and relevant.

Incorporating regular life audits into your yearly routine ensures continuous personal growth and aligns your life's direction with your deepest values and aspirations. It empowers you to make informed decisions, build resilience against adversity, and cultivate a lifestyle that not only meets but exceeds your expectations of fulfillment and success. Revisit your audit frequently to track progress, celebrate achievements, and reassess priorities, ensuring that your life's journey remains vibrant and meaningful.

Reflecting on each area of your life becomes a powerful exercise in mindfulness. As you rate your satisfaction across categories like career, finances, mental and physical health, friendships, and hobbies, patterns emerge that guide further action. Take note if certain aspects consistently rate lower than others; these may require dedicated effort and resources for improvement. Conversely, acknowledge and seek to replicate strategies where satisfaction is high, transferring successful behaviors to other areas needing attention.

The revelations that emerge from a thorough life review enable the setting of intentions — ways of living that steer day-to-day choices. Intentions like fostering kindness, practicing gratitude, or enhancing emotional intelligence shape behavior in subtle yet impactful ways. These commitments complement specific goals, creating a holistic approach to personal growth. Display your intentions prominently, reminding yourself daily of the broader principles guiding your life journey.

Navigating the complexities of modern life requires tools that offer both guidance and adaptability. Regular life audits are a proactive measure, equipping young adults, students, and professionals to thrive amid life's demands. They serve as a beacon, illuminating the path to a well-rounded, fulfilling existence that honors one's core values and dreams.

Reflect on Past Mistakes as Learning Opportunities

Turning mistakes into stepping stones for personal growth begins with altering the way we perceive errors. Rather than approaching them with self-condemnation, we can shift our mindset to understand that mistakes are a natural part of the learning process. By seeing mistakes through a constructive lens, we transform what might initially feel like defeat into opportunities for development. This change in perspective fosters resilience and helps us grow more confident in tackling future challenges.

Consider how changing this narrative can have positive effects on your mental health and outlook on life. For instance, if you've ever felt overwhelmed by an error at work or school, acknowledging it as a chance to learn can reduce stress and anxiety. When embraced with a growth mindset, even significant setbacks can become lessons that drive personal improvement.

Identifying key takeaways from our mistakes is crucial in utilizing them for growth. Reflective questions serve as a powerful tool here. Ask yourself: What went wrong? Why did it happen? What could I do differently next time? Diving into these questions allows you to extract valuable insights and contribute to improved decision-making going forward (Wright, 2023). A practical approach is to maintain a reflective journal where you document your mistakes and the lessons learned from each. Over time, reviewing this collection of experiences can illustrate how much you've grown and help guide your future choices.

Moreover, sharing experiences of mistakes with others can be profoundly beneficial. When you communicate your lessons with peers, not only do you solidify your understanding, but you also create an opportunity for collective learning. A supportive community often leads to richer insights as different perspectives come into play. Suppose you're part of a study group or workplace team; discussing mistakes openly can foster an environment of mutual learning and support, making everyone involved more adept at handling similar situations in the future.

In addition, fostering the habit of sharing helps break down barriers of isolation that mistakes sometimes build around us. Knowing that others have faced similar challenges and emerged stronger can be incredibly reassuring. It also opens up pathways for mentorship, wherein someone else's insights can offer new strategies and ways of thinking that you may not have considered.

Practicing self-compassion plays an integral role when reflecting on past errors. Often, we're our own harshest critics when we make mistakes. However, treating oneself with kindness and understanding during these times is vital for maintaining motivation and resilience. Imagine speaking to yourself the way you would comfort a friend facing difficulty—this simple shift can help mitigate feelings of frustration and inadequacy.

By adopting self-compassionate practices, you create a nurturing internal environment, essential for growth. Instead of lingering on what went wrong, focus on how far you've come and your progress. Reinforce this mindset by celebrating small victories along the way, further boosting morale and encouraging perseverance through trials.

Letting go of the notion of perfectionism is equally important. Remember, everyone makes mistakes; they don't define who you are, but rather contribute to who you're becoming. The willingness to make mistakes—and learn from them—sets the stage for true innovation and creativity in all areas of life.

Celebrate Small Victories to Build Self-Esteem

Recognizing even small achievements is crucial in building a sense of triumph and setting the stage for larger successes. This practice of acknowledging little victories boosts our confidence and fuels motivation, allowing us to approach bigger challenges with increased self-assurance. The psychology behind celebrating minor accomplishments lies in the reinforcement of positive behaviors. When you recognize your efforts, no matter how insignificant they may seem, you validate your hard work and perseverance. This can be compared to laying the bricks that eventually form the foundation of a sturdy building — each brick is vital for the integrity of the entire structure. As noted by the Mind Tools Content Team (2022), keeping track of and celebrating these small wins helps in maintaining momentum, making it easier to progress toward more substantial goals.

Once you appreciate the importance of celebrating small accomplishments, exploring different methods to do so is a natural next step. Celebrations don't always have to be grand; they can be simple acts that provide a sense of reward. Giving yourself a treat after completing a project or sharing your success with friends on social media are effective ways to acknowledge your progress. Social sharing, in particular, not only lets others know about your achievements but also welcomes their encouragement, reinforcing the behavior further. Consider making a list of potential rewards that resonate with you — perhaps a relaxing evening with your favorite movie, a special meal, or indulging in a hobby. Celebrating in this way turns the act of recognition into something tangible and enjoyable. By integrating celebration into your routine, you create a positive feedback loop that strengthens your resolve to continue striving for success.

Maintaining an achievement log is another powerful tool in the arsenal of personal growth. An achievement log serves as a written record of your accomplishments, providing tangible evidence of your ongoing progress. During challenging times, this log can be a source of motivation, reminding you of past successes and your capacity to overcome obstacles. When negativity creeps in, or when you face setbacks, revisiting your achievement log can boost your self-esteem and renew your determination to push forward. Keeping a log doesn't require elaborate effort — a simple notebook or a digital document where you jot down each milestone, no matter its size, will suffice. According to the research published in Why Teachers and Students Should Celebrate Their Successes: Boosting Confidence and Building Momentum (2023), tracking successes not only marks progress but also becomes a powerful motivator for further growth. It's like having a journal of positivity that you can turn to whenever you need a lift.

Creating guidelines for effectively maintaining an achievement log can enhance its usefulness. Start by establishing a dedicated space for recording your achievements, whether it's a specific app, a diary, or a section in your planner. Regularly update the log, ideally at the end of each day or week, while the details are still fresh. Capture not just what you achieved, but also how you felt about it, any challenges you overcame, and lessons learned. Reflect periodically on your entries to gain insights into patterns and progress over time. This reflective process adds depth to the log, transforming it from a simple list into a tool for personal development.

Fostering a supportive environment plays a key role in

celebrating successes. Involving friends and family in your celebrations can strengthen bonds and create a sense of community. Sharing your achievements with those who care about you enhances feelings of warmth and connection. These loved ones can offer congratulations and encouragement, contributing to a collective joy that magnifies the experience. Moreover, involving others can sometimes offer new perspectives, helping you see value in your victories that you might have otherwise overlooked. Encouraging them to share their triumphs fosters a reciprocal relationship where everyone uplifts each other, creating a network of support that boosts collective confidence and enriches personal growth journeys.

Guidelines for fostering this supportive environment can include organizing regular get-togethers, either virtually or in-person, where accomplishments are shared and celebrated. Setting a positive tone during these gatherings – focusing on encouragement rather than competition – enhances the atmosphere of support. Encourage storytelling: let each person share the journey leading to their success, which adds context and emotion, making celebrations more meaningful. Acknowledge both individual and group achievements, as collective successes can be especially empowering. Remember, the goal is to create a safe and nurturing space that celebrates individuality and fosters unity.

Summary and Reflections

Reflective practices like journaling and life audits are powerful tools for enhancing self-awareness and personal development. Journaling gives you the chance to express your emotions and gather your thoughts, leading to greater clarity about yourself and your experiences. It's a way to set goals and track your progress, offering motivation even during challenging times. Using prompts can dive deeper into your introspective journey, helping young adults, college students, and professionals unlock insights about themselves. Meanwhile, reviewing past entries creates a feedback loop that showcases growth over time. Life audits complement this by prompting intentional reflection on life's various aspects. They allow you to evaluate your current situation against your values and long-term goals, pushing you to make informed decisions about where you want to head next.

These reflective practices guide you in turning past mistakes into valuable learning opportunities. Embracing errors with a constructive mindset nurtures resilience and paves the way for personal growth. By reflecting on mistakes, you can identify key takeaways that enhance your decision-making skills. Sharing these experiences with others fosters a community of mutual support and collective learning. Additionally, celebrating small victories builds self-esteem and strengthens your resolve. Recognizing minor achievements not only boosts confidence but also fuels motivation, encouraging you to tackle bigger challenges. With consistency and an open heart, these practices empower you to navigate adulthood's demands while maintaining focus on personal growth and fulfillment.

14

Navigating Friendships and Peer Influence

Managing Peer Influence and Nurturing Authentic Friendships

Managing peer influence and nurturing authentic friendships is a journey young adults often find themselves navigating as they step into adulthood. Crafting one's identity amidst the myriad voices of peers while fostering genuine relationships can feel like a balancing act. In these pivotal years, friends play an influential role, becoming mirrors reflecting our aspirations, fears, and values. It's in this space that we learn who encourages us, who listens, and who truly has our best interests at heart. Through understanding and intentional actions, it's possible to cultivate friendships that contribute to personal growth and positive community dynamics. The bond of true friendships not only enhances our social lives but also strengthens our mental well-being, providing a sturdy support system during life's ups and downs.

In this chapter, we delve into strategies for maintaining individuality within group dynamics, encouraging readers to reflect on their own values and boundaries. We explore how to evaluate peer influences thoughtfully, ensuring decisions align with personal beliefs rather than external pressures. By examining specific scenarios related to daily social interactions, readers will gain insights into transforming awareness into actionable steps. Furthermore, the chapter provides practical tips on setting and respecting personal boundaries, illustrating how effective communication reinforces mutual respect in friendships. This exploration extends to contributing positively to communities, highlighting the importance of finding shared goals that foster meaningful engagements. Finally, integrating authenticity with adaptability is discussed, helping young adults balance the diverse demands of friendships and societal expectations. Through narrative examples and relatable guidance, the chapter aims to equip readers with the tools to navigate their social worlds confidently and meaningfully.

Identify Characteristics of Supportive Friendships

Recognizing qualities that define healthy friendships is crucial for anyone looking to build meaningful and supportive relationships. One of the most vital traits in a high-quality friendship is trustworthiness. This quality forms the backbone of reliable connections, ensuring that friends can depend on each other no matter the circumstance. Trustworthiness encompasses honesty, confidentiality, and respect for boundaries. A trustworthy friend is someone who treats your secrets with care and respects your personal space, creating a safe environment where you feel comfortable being vulnerable. They maintain integrity by aligning their actions with their promises, showing that they value your trust. Building this type of relationship requires both parties to be consistent and transparent, laying a foundation that can withstand the tests of time and trials.

An encouraging nature is another essential characteristic of healthy friendships. Friends should uplift each other, provide support during challenging times, and celebrate successes together. An encouraging friend sees potential in you that you might not see in yourself; they inspire you to strive for better and reassure you when you're doubtful. Encouragement doesn't mean blind agreement; rather, it involves constructive feedback that fosters personal growth and boosts self-confidence. When friends cultivate an uplifting atmosphere, they strengthen their bond, making each interaction a source of motivation and joy. This mutual encouragement creates a dynamic where both individuals contribute to each other's development, enabling them to pursue personal ambitions while feeling empowered by the support of their friend.

Active listening is another cornerstone of effective and healthy friendships. It goes beyond just hearing words; it's about fully engaging in conversations and responding empathetically. Active listeners validate emotions, enhancing understanding between friends. By paying full attention and acknowledging what a friend says, you make them feel valued and heard. This attentiveness aids in resolving conflicts by addressing misunderstandings before they escalate into major disputes. Engaging in active listening can also deepen emotional connections, as it demonstrates that you genuinely care about your friend's feelings and perspectives. Practicing this form of communication cultivates empathy and patience, key components that enable friendships to thrive amidst disagreements or challenges.

Supporting mutual growth within friendships is equally important. Healthy friendships are characterized by a balance where both friends experience personal growth and pursue shared goals. This mutual dedication to development strengthens the commitment between the two individuals. Supporting each other's personal ambitions ensures that each person feels valued not only for who they are but also for who they aspire to become. When friendships foster an environment conducive to growth, they promote learning opportunities and expand experiences that enrich both parties' lives. Encouraging one another's aspirations and celebrating achievements reflects a deep-seated investment in the friendship itself. Such friendships often result in stronger commitments, as they are based on shared dreams and long-term visions that are built through collaboration and mutual encouragement.

The essence of recognizing these qualities lies in understanding the positive impact they have on overall mental and emotional wellbeing. Research consistently highlights how high-quality friendships enhance resilience against stress and anxiety while boosting self-esteem and cognitive health (*11 Unique Traits That Define a Truly High-Quality Friend, According to Psychology*, 2024). For young adults navigating the complexities of adulthood, nurturing such relationships can offer a solid support system that eases the burdens of personal and professional life challenges. As college students seek practical methods to handle academic pressures and young professionals focus on work-life balance, understanding the value of trustworthy, encouraging, actively listening, and growth-focused friendships becomes even more critical.

Evaluate the Influence of Your Peer Group on Your Choices

Navigating the challenges of adulthood often means learning to manage peer pressure while maintaining a sense of self. For many young adults, this means developing a keen awareness of how peers influence everyday decisions. Becoming aware of peer pressure can indeed aid in making decisions that are more aligned with personal values. Understanding peer dynamics requires reflection on one's behavior and the way social interactions shape choices.

Peer pressure is an omnipresent force. It can subtly mold our preferences, sometimes without us even realizing it. Acknowledging its presence is the first step towards conscious decision-making. When individuals recognize the impact of peer pressure, they can start aligning their choices with personal values rather than merely conforming to group expectations. Being aware helps maintain individuality and ensures that one's actions reflect their true self, rather than simply seeking validation from others (Cruz, 2024).

For instance, consider a situation where a young professional faces pressure to participate in after-work gatherings that involve heavy drinking. An individual who understands peer pressure might choose to attend but decide beforehand not to drink excessively, thereby prioritizing their health over fitting in. This kind of awareness allows for decisions that are not only socially informed but also grounded in personal beliefs.

Behavior reflection is another crucial component of managing peer influence. Reflecting on one's actions helps assess whether these align with personal values. Such introspection offers insights into friendship dynamics, revealing which relationships genuinely support an individual's growth and integrity. By examining past interactions and the emotions they evoke, individuals can identify patterns that might need adjustment.

Imagine a college student who starts skipping classes because friends deem academics 'uncool.' On reflecting, this student realizes that academic success aligns more closely with personal values than momentary social approval. Through introspection, the student gains clarity, allowing them to reassess priorities and make changes conducive to long-term goals.

Alongside awareness and reflection, analyzing the consequences of one's actions is vital. A thoughtful examination of potential outcomes promotes accountability and encourages careful consideration before making decisions. This approach helps in evaluating whether peer-influenced decisions are worth pursuing or if they might lead to negative ramifications like stress or guilt.

Consider a scenario where a young adult feels pressured to join in spreading rumors about a colleague. By analyzing potential consequences, they may realize how such actions could harm the workplace atmosphere or damage reputations. Viewing the situation through a lens of accountability prompts deeper self-assessment, leading to more responsible conduct.

Establishing healthy boundaries is paramount in mitigating the adverse effects of peer pressure. Setting firm limits protects personal integrity and reduces exposure to negative influences. Boundaries signify respect for oneself and communicate to others what behaviors are acceptable. They serve as a protective buffer, ensuring interactions remain respectful and balanced.

For example, a young adult might feel the need to continuously respond to texts or calls from friends, fearing abandonment if they don't. By setting boundaries around communication times, they convey a need for personal space. Such limits prevent encroachment on personal time and reduce anxiety.

Creating these boundaries can be challenging yet empowering. It's important to remember that personal happiness and well-being should take precedence over pleasing others. While peers play a significant role in shaping experiences, individual perspectives and ideals should guide decisions.

Maintain Individuality Amidst Group Dynamics

Retaining your unique identity in social groups can be both challenging and rewarding. It's about understanding who you are and valuing that individual self while effectively engaging with others. Let's explore how to do this, beginning with the power of self-reflection.

Self-reflection is a cornerstone of self-awareness, guiding our decisions and interactions. By regularly setting aside time to think deeply about your values, strengths, and weaknesses, you cultivate a clearer sense of who you are. This process of introspection could involve journaling, meditation, or simply pondering your thoughts during a quiet moment. Through consistent self-reflection, you gain insights into what truly matters to you, helping navigate life's complexities with clarity and purpose. Becoming aware of patterns and emotions enhances self-understanding and aids in aligning your actions with your core beliefs (Wright, 2023).

On the path of nurturing genuine connections, embracing social authenticity is vital. Authenticity encourages relationships built on mutual respect and honesty. When you're authentic, you're not putting up a facade or conforming just to fit in; instead, you offer your true self to the world. This transparency fosters trust, as people feel they know who you genuinely are. Moreover, it invites others to reciprocate with their own authenticity, leading to more meaningful interactions. It's like peeling away layers to reveal the real you and allowing others to appreciate you for who you truly are.

Creative self-expression serves as an empowering tool to highlight individuality and enrich life experiences. Whether through art, music, writing, or even fashion choices, expressing yourself creatively allows others to see the world through your unique lens. The act of creating is not only fulfilling but also opens new avenues of emotional release and selfdiscovery. In addition, exploring different forms of creative expression can lead to increased self-esteem and well-being, as your self-concept aligns closely with how you present yourself to the world (What Is Self-Expression? Why Does It Matter?, n.d.). By sharing your individuality, you enhance not just your own life, but also those of others around you.

Finding a balance between adaptability and authenticity is crucial in maintaining your unique identity while being part of a group. Adaptability doesn't mean altering who you are; rather, it's about being open to different viewpoints and experiences without losing sight of your own values. This flexibility allows you to engage constructively in diverse environments. However, it's equally important to remain firm on issues and values that define you. This balance strengthens resolve and sustains mutual respect within friendships, allowing you to stay true to yourself while respecting the identities of others.

Guidelines for implementing these practices effectively can transform abstract ideals into practical habits that foster a balanced sense of self. For self-reflection, consider establishing a regular routine—perhaps a weekly journaling session or daily moments of mindful meditation. This practice ensures you continuously tune into your inner feelings and thoughts, keeping you aligned with your true self. Additionally, engaging in open conversations with trusted friends or mentors can provide feedback and different perspectives that might inspire further self-awareness. For balancing adaptability and authenticity, try establishing personal boundaries. Know when to stand your ground and when to flex, ensuring that your essential values remain intact even as you explore new ideas and opportunities.

Contribute Positively to Your Communities

In today's fast-paced world, fostering community interactions comes with immense rewards. Community engagement serves as a cornerstone in enhancing our sense of belonging and fulfillment. Imagine attending a local event—the shared laughter, the friendly nods, and small talk that eventually blooms into friendships. These connections are not just momentary; they weave a tapestry of purpose and identity. By engaging with your community, you find yourself intertwined in a network where each knot and thread supports and uplifts the other, binding everyone closer together.

Positive actions within communities can create ripples that inspire others to act similarly, leading to an environment built on resilience and support. Imagine volunteering at a food bank or participating in a neighborhood cleanup. Your efforts can encourage others to join, creating a chain reaction of goodwill and cooperation. Each positive action contributes to building a community that's more than just a geographical location—it's a supportive network where people look out for one another. It's about setting examples, where kindness and responsibility influence others to do the same. This sense of mutual inspiration fosters an environment where each member feels valued and empowered to contribute further.

Volunteerism acts as a powerful vehicle for boosting empathy, expanding social networks, and enhancing mental health through purposeful activities. When you volunteer, you step into another person's shoes and see life from their perspective, fostering empathy and understanding. A study by Western Connecticut State University (2018) highlights that volunteering establishes strong community ties and broadens your social network. It introduces you to individuals who share similar interests and values, thus creating lasting bonds and friendships. Engaging with such diverse groups enhances your social and relationship skills, making you more adept at navigating different social dynamics.

Furthermore, the mental health benefits of volunteering are undeniable. As per research outlined by Thoreson (2023), engaging in volunteer activities improves both physical and mental health, especially among older adults. Such activities reduce stress levels, elevate mood, and provide a sense of accomplishment. The act of giving back not only benefits those you help but profoundly impacts your own well-being, nurturing feelings of happiness and satisfaction.

Building support networks around shared values also deepens meaningful engagement within communities. These networks often arise from collective goals or missions that resonate with the members involved. Take, for instance, a community garden project. Everyone involved shares a commitment to sustainability and healthy living. Working towards this common goal strengthens relationships and boosts engagement. The collaboration involved requires communication techniques to ensure all voices are heard and considered, promoting inclusivity and respect.

Moreover, managing reactions becomes crucial in maintaining harmony within these networks. Different perspectives and ideas can lead to disagreements, and it's important to address these constructively. For instance, during a collaborative project, if someone disagrees with the proposed direction, using effective communication techniques, like active listening and empathetic responses, can help manage the situation gracefully.

Reinforcing boundaries within community engagements is essential. While working closely with others, it's vital to establish what works for you and align your contributions accordingly. This might mean knowing when to assertively say no to overcommitting or clarifying roles to avoid conflicts. Clear boundaries enable you to give your best without feeling overwhelmed, contributing to a healthy balance between personal needs and community involvement.

Expanding on the role of shared values, consider how initiatives centered on environmental causes can unite people with diverse backgrounds. Volunteers participating in beach cleanups or tree planting events come with varied experiences, yet they're unified by their dedication to the cause. This common ground creates opportunities for exchanging ideas and learning from one another, enriching the experience for everyone involved.

Engaging with your community isn't just about one-off events or short-term projects. It's about cultivating ongoing relationships and laying the groundwork for a community spirit that persists beyond immediate needs. Particularly for young adults and college students, these engagements offer a constructive outlet to navigate adulthood's emotional and social challenges. They learn to manage emotions and balance life's demands while being a part of something bigger than themselves, nurturing both personal growth and communal ties.

The drive to connect, belong, and contribute positively to a community is engrained in us. We thrive in environments where we feel accepted and understood. As young professionals, the workspace often becomes our primary community. Here, engaging positively can bolster workplace satisfaction and self-care. Contributing to team efforts, participating in work-led community service initiatives, or even organizing group activities can enhance team synergy and personal fulfillment.

Summary and Reflections

In this chapter, we've explored how important it is to understand and nurture qualities that make friendships supportive and meaningful. We've talked about trustworthiness as the foundation of any strong friendship, where honesty and respect build a reliable connection between friends. Encouragement plays a key role, as uplifting each other helps us grow and face challenges confidently. Active listening also proves essential, allowing us to truly connect with our friends by valuing their thoughts and feelings. By focusing on mutual growth, we ensure friendships not only survive but thrive, offering us a safe space for personal development. Recognizing these characteristics can significantly enhance our mental and emotional well-being, providing a support network that eases life's pressures.

Moving beyond individuals, the chapter highlights evaluating peer influence, maintaining individuality, and contributing positively to communities. Navigating peer pressure with awareness helps us make choices aligned with our true selves rather than mere conformity. Establishing boundaries protects personal integrity and encourages healthy social interactions. Meanwhile, self-reflection and authenticity aid in preserving individuality within group dynamics, ensuring we're genuine in how we present ourselves. Engaging actively in our communities fosters belonging and allows us to impact others positively through actions rooted in shared values. Together, these strategies equip young adults, college students, and young professionals with tools needed to lead balanced lives filled with authentic relationships and deeper community connections.

15

Creating a Vision Board for Success

Harnessing the Power of Vision Boards

Creating vision boards is an engaging way for young adults to clarify their goals and visualize their desired future. The process goes beyond merely crafting a collage; it taps into one's creativity and helps establish a tangible representation of personal ambitions. As individuals embark on various life stages—whether pursuing higher education, starting a career, or managing relationships—vision boards emerge as supportive tools in navigating these transitions. By assembling meaningful images and symbols, young people can cultivate a deeper connection with their aspirations, encouraging them to dream bigger and aim higher.

In this chapter, we will explore the practical steps involved in creating a vision board and delve into how this creative exercise can serve as a powerful manifestation tool. From selecting the right materials that resonate with your personal style to finding inspiration from diverse sources, each stage of the process enhances clarity about what's truly important. We'll discuss how incorporating personalized text and symbolic elements can deepen the significance of your board, acting as affirmations and reminders of your path. Additionally, we'll cover the benefits of regularly updating your board to keep it aligned with your evolving goals. By sharing your vision board with trusted individuals, you can foster a supportive network committed to mutual encouragement and success. Through these discussions, the chapter aims to inspire readers to embrace vision boards as dynamic maps guiding them toward a fulfilling and balanced life.

Gather Materials that Symbolize Your Ambitions

Vision boards have become a popular tool for young adults to manifest their dreams and set clear goals. Creating one can be an enriching exercise that channels creativity while providing clarity. To start, it's essential to choose the right physical or digital board that matches your individual style yet remains practical in terms of visibility. A board hidden away won't serve its purpose, so balance personal aesthetic preferences with accessibility. This could mean opting for a vibrant poster board in your workspace or crafting a sleek digital version on a platform like Canva, designed with easily changeable layers.

Once you've chosen your medium, move on to collecting images, quotes, and words that truly resonate with your goals. The source of these elements can vary—from old magazines to curated Pinterest boards, all offering a wealth of visual inspiration. Seek out materials that evoke strong emotions tied to your aspirations. For instance, if your goal is to travel more, look for images of destinations you dream of visiting, infused with colors and scenes that fill you with a sense of wanderlust. Diversify your sources to capture different aspects of your aspirations (Perry, 2023).

Another powerful facet of vision boards is incorporating personalized text and symbols. Words have power, and when they affirm core desires, they can significantly motivate. Consider adding text that embodies what you wish to manifest, whether through bold declarations like "I am capable" or subtle reminders such as "peace." Utilize symbols which speak to you personally—perhaps a small drawing of an open door symbolizing new opportunities or a heart representing love and compassion. These elements can imbue your board with deeper meaning and act as triggers for positive thoughts whenever you view them (Wright, 2023).

Assembling these collected materials requires engaging with your creativity, making the process both therapeutic and grounding. How you lay out your vision board should feel natural and intentional. Arrange your images and text in ways that make you excited about the future: use grids for organized thinkers or allow a more free-form approach for artistic minds. Play with textures by layering different paper types or adding tactile elements such as fabric swatches or pressed flowers. This stage isn't just about aesthetics; it's an opportunity to refine your vision and connect more deeply with your goals.

Once your board takes shape, find a prominent spot where it'll catch your eye daily, reinforcing your ambitions with regularity. Keep in mind that your vision board isn't static. Goals evolve, and your board should too. Update it as needed, swapping out outdated visuals for new ones that reflect your current path. This ongoing interaction keeps the momentum alive, encouraging you to stay engaged with your aspirations.

Sharing your vision board with trusted individuals can further enhance its impact. Whether it's with a roommate, partner, or close friend, discussing your goals opens avenues for support and accountability. Their understanding of your vision can foster shared encouragement and perhaps even inspire collaborative efforts towards mutual dreams.

In crafting your vision board, remember it is more than just art; it's a reflection of your dreams—a dynamic map guiding you through life's journey. It should evolve as you do, portraying the ebb and flow of your aspirations, helping you visualize not only where you are going but also reminding you of how far you've come. By regularly revisiting and updating it, you'll maintain a fresh perspective on your goals, ensuring that your board continues to align with your ever-growing ambitions.

Regularly Update Your Vision Board to Stay Inspired

When embarking on the journey of self-discovery and growth through vision boards, it's vital to remember the power of revisiting and refreshing these visual tools regularly. A vision board is more than just a collage of aspirations; it is a dynamic canvas that mirrors our evolving goals and ambitions. As we navigate different phases in life, our priorities may shift, making it necessary to update our vision boards to stay aligned with our personal growth. This process not only keeps us motivated but also validates our journey toward self-improvement.

Recognizing that our goals are not static is the first step in maintaining an effective vision board. As young adults and professionals juggle various responsibilities, their dreams can change direction. Whether it's a career goal, a relationship aspiration, or a personal milestone, acknowledging this fluidity encourages us to revisit our vision boards actively. Refreshing these boards allows for an honest reflection of where we stand and what truly matters to us now. This constant evolution ensures that the board remains relevant and continues to inspire us every day.

One practical way to maintain this relevance is by scheduling routine check-ins. Setting aside time at regular intervals—be it monthly or quarterly—to evaluate our boards can reignite the excitement about our dreams. These sessions act as powerful reminders of why we embarked on particular paths and what outcomes we aim to manifest. Moreover, routine check-ins enhance accountability. By consistently reviewing our boards, we engage in a reflective dialogue with ourselves, asking crucial questions like "Am I moving towards these goals?" or "Do these dreams still reflect my true desires?" This practice helps in identifying any discrepancies between our current actions and desired outcomes, providing a clearer roadmap for future efforts.

To further breathe life into our vision boards, introducing new inspirations can be remarkably beneficial. Life is full of serendipitous moments and unforeseen opportunities that inspire us unexpectedly. Incorporating fresh elements on our boards—perhaps a newly discovered quote, an image that stirs emotion, or even a symbol representing a newfound interest—can rekindle creativity and affirm the progress we have made so far. Not only does this keep the board visually and emotionally stimulating, but it also serves as a narrative of our journey, showcasing how each piece added represents another stepping stone on our path.

Creating a reflection space dedicated to contemplation

around your vision board is another invaluable practice. In our fast-paced lives, having a serene spot where we can sit, relax, and connect with our aspirations strengthens our bond with our visions. This space doesn't have to be elaborate—a comfortable chair by a window, a cushion in a quiet corner, or even sitting cross-legged on the floor by the board. What matters is the intention behind it: taking a pause from the chaos of daily life to refocus on what truly matters to us. Such reflection allows us to delve deeper into understanding our motivations and challenges, fostering a stronger connection with our aspirations.

As we revisit and refresh our vision boards, it's also important to celebrate the milestones we achieve along the way. Every goal accomplished, no matter how small, deserves acknowledgment. This celebration could be as simple as updating the board with a photo taken during a trip you had once envisioned or adding a congratulatory note to yourself for achieving a professional landmark. Celebrating achievements aligns with cultivating a positive mindset and boosts confidence, reinforcing our belief in the power of visualization and manifestation.

Furthermore, one must remain open to the idea of letting go of certain images or goals that no longer resonate. This act of decluttering paves the way for new opportunities and possibilities. It's perfectly normal for some aspects of the vision board to lose significance over time. By removing these elements, we create space for more meaningful and purposeful goals that match our current aspirations. This process of elimination is not about failure but about conscious growth and adaptation.

For many, incorporating positive affirmations alongside

visual elements on their boards has been transformative. These affirmations, when reviewed regularly, can shape our thought processes, turning self-doubt into empowerment. Coupled with visualization, affirmations reinforce our commitment to our dreams and bolster our mental resolve to pursue them actively.

In conclusion, vision boards hold immense potential to guide us through the ebbs and flows of life, especially for young adults finding their footing in adulthood. They are not just artistic creations but living strategies that require nurturing and attention. Revisiting and refreshing these boards instills discipline, cultivates motivation, and reflects our ever-evolving selves. By embracing changes, celebrating successes, and creating spaces for reflection, we transform our vision board from a mere collection of images into a compelling, ongoing narrative of our life's journey.

Use Visualization Techniques to Fortify Belief in Goals

Visualization is more than just a technique; it's a powerful tool that young adults can harness to cultivate motivation and belief in their personal and professional goals. At its core, visualization involves practicing detailed mental imagery to vividly picture success, and this practice fosters a sense of ownership over one's aspirations. For those navigating the often overwhelming transitions of entering adulthood, employing such mental techniques can create a clear path toward achieving desired outcomes.

The journey begins with practicing detailed mental imagery—an essential component for visualizing success. By creating a vivid mental picture of your future achievements, you effectively carve out a path to follow. This technique is not reserved solely for athletes or high-performing individuals but is accessible to anyone seeking clarity and direction. Imagine a college student, stressed about exams and career prospects, who spends a few moments each day imagining themselves at their dream job, excelling and feeling accomplished. This process instills confidence and provides a tangible representation of what might otherwise seem nebulous.

Incorporating all senses into your visualization greatly enhances its effectiveness. This immersion makes the visualization experience more realistic and believable, anchoring the desired outcome in your subconscious mind. Picture yourself not only seeing but also hearing, smelling, and even tasting elements of your future environment. If your goal is to travel abroad for work, imagine the sound of a bustling foreign market, the aroma of local cuisine, and the tactile experience of handling new currencies. Engaging all senses can make the vision more compelling and attainable, enhancing belief in possibilities (Canfield, 2020).

Integrating visualization exercises into daily routines can substantially reinforce your goals. Like brushing your teeth each morning or stretching before bed, visualization should become a regular ritual. Set aside dedicated time, whether it's during a morning coffee or a quiet moment before sleep, to immerse yourself in your mental imagery. Consistent practice keeps your goals prominent in your mind and motivates you to take small yet meaningful steps towards achieving them. The regular reinforcement of these images serves as a reminder of your capabilities and potential, guiding everyday decisions and actions.

Guidelines for incorporating visualization into daily life

can be beneficial. Consider establishing a specific time and environment that supports relaxation and focus. Perhaps establish a morning routine where you visualize your tasks for the day, centering your intention on positive outcomes. A visualization exercise could involve sitting quietly, closing your eyes, and diving deep into the mental image you have constructed, engaging each sense as vividly as possible. Over time, this repetition strengthens the mental pathways leading towards your goals and helps maintain your motivation even when faced with obstacles (lifecoachtraining, 2023).

Aligning positive self-talk with visualization is also critical in countering doubts and building confidence. The dialogue we maintain with ourselves significantly impacts our mindset and belief systems. When paired with visualization, affirmations can reinforce confidence and dispel negative thoughts. As you visualize, accompany the process with affirmations such as "I am capable of reaching my goals" or "Every step I take brings me closer to success." These statements act as verbal anchors, reinforcing the mental images and supporting the belief in your potential.

In visualization, guidelines again play an important role. It involves consciously choosing affirmations that resonate personally and reflect genuine aspirations. Begin with simple, honest statements that align with the mental images you've created. Repeat these affirmations during visualization sessions to strengthen the connection between your beliefs and actions. This practice not only builds resilience against external doubts but also cultivates a proactive mindset focused on progress.

For example, consider a young professional aiming for a promotion at work. Alongside visualizing themselves excelling in their desired role, they use affirmations like "I am ready and prepared for new challenges" to underpin their ambitions. Gradually, they begin to notice a shift in behavior—taking initiative in projects, volunteering for leadership roles, and displaying increased confidence in meetings. These changes stem from aligning their visualization with positive self-talk, creating a feedback loop that fosters growth and goal attainment.

Display the Board Where You'll See It Daily and Share Your Vision

The power of vision boards lies not only in their creation but also in strategic placement, which can significantly enhance their effectiveness. To ensure that these visual goals become a staple of daily life, it's vital to choose a spot where the board is frequently seen. This decision should be guided by your daily habits and routines—whether it's above a workspace, near a mirror you use often, or even as a screensaver on your device if digital. The constant exposure to these images helps embed them into your subconscious, reinforcing your ambitions every time you glance at the board. The goal is to make it as unavoidable as brushing your teeth; it becomes a part of your everyday existence, aiding in the affirmation of your goals (Dartnell, 2021).

Creating a dedicated space surrounding your vision board can amplify its inspirational impact. Think of this area as more than just a location for your board; consider it an altar to your future self. This space could include motivational quotes, a cozy chair where you engage in thoughtful reflection, or perhaps a small shelf with tokens that represent milestones you've reached. The aim is to cultivate a ritualized environment that draws you in and encourages regular interaction. When designed thoughtfully, this space acts not just as storage for dreams, but as a catalyst for ambition, setting a tone for aspiration-led rituals that further anchor your goals in reality.

Incorporating reminders or triggers plays a pivotal role in keeping your connection to the vision board consistent. These reminders might take the form of alarms or notifications set at regular intervals, prompting you to spend a few minutes focused on your board each day. You could schedule these interactions during moments when you're likely to need a motivational boost, such as before tackling challenging tasks or after returning from work. Over time, these triggers help sustain your focus on aspirations, ensuring that your goals remain top of mind amidst life's distractions. They remind you to take deliberate pauses and reflect on your journey, maintaining momentum towards your desired outcomes.

While placing and personalizing your vision board are individual activities, sharing your vision within a community can create additional layers of accountability and encouragement. Engaging friends, family, or colleagues in discussions about your vision board can open up opportunities for support and collaboration. For instance, you might describe some of the goals represented on your board during casual conversations or share progress updates on social media, inviting feedback and support. Though this isn't a strict requirement, doing so can foster a sense of shared purpose and mutual inspiration. The gentle pressure of knowing others are aware of your ambitions can motivate you to stay committed, pushing past obstacles and celebrating wins together (Darian D, 2020).

Concluding Thoughts

Vision boards serve as a vibrant canvas, helping young adults manifest dreams and clarify goals. As explored in this chapter, the journey of building a vision board starts with gathering materials that symbolize individual aspirations, turning abstract desires into tangible visuals. These boards are more than just collections of images; they act as dynamic tools for self-discovery, driving motivation and providing clarity on one's path. By thoughtfully selecting symbols and words that resonate with personal ambitions, young adults can create a map that guides them through the varied landscape of adulthood. Engaging with this creative process can be both therapeutic and grounding, allowing individuals to connect deeply with their future selves.

Regularly interacting with your vision board keeps your intentions alive and evolving. It's an ongoing conversation with yourself, reminding you not just of where you want to go but also honoring how far you've come. As life changes, so should your board; updating it ensures that what inspires you today reflects current goals and dreams. Sharing your board with trusted friends or family can add layers of support, making your journey collaborative. By maintaining a fresh perspective and celebrating small victories along the way, vision boards transform from mere artistic expression into powerful narratives of growth and self-discovery.

16

Your Journey Toward Continuous Growth

Sustaining Growth and Maintaining Momentum

Sustaining growth and maintaining momentum in personal and professional lives is an ongoing endeavor that hinges on our ability to learn and adapt. In a world where change is the only constant, embracing lifelong learning becomes more than just an academic pursuit; it turns into a vital survival skill. It's about cultivating a mindset open to new experiences and ideas, which allows us to tackle challenges head-on and emerge stronger. As we navigate through our careers and personal journeys, the capacity to evolve becomes a cornerstone of resilience, empowering us to seize new opportunities and flourish amid uncertainty.

This chapter delves into the art of nurturing continuous development by focusing on lifelong learning and resilience-building strategies. Readers will explore how to integrate learning seamlessly into everyday life, utilizing diverse resources like online courses and community interactions. The narrative unfolds with practical insights into transforming routine moments into learning opportunities, amplifying both personal and professional competencies. Additionally, the chapter sheds light on embracing change as a positive force, transforming it from a source of anxiety into a stepping stone for personal growth. By engaging with the topics covered here, individuals are guided towards harnessing their full potential, setting them on a path to sustained success and personal fulfillment.

Commit to Lifelong Learning and Adaptability

In today's rapidly evolving world, sustaining personal and professional growth demands a commitment to continuous learning and adaptability. To thrive amidst constant change, adopting a mindset that embraces lifelong learning is essential. This approach not only secures competitiveness in the job market but also enhances resilience in the face of challenges.

One fundamental step towards fostering continuous growth is establishing a habit of regular learning through diverse educational formats. The modern learner has access to an abundance of resources, ranging from online courses and virtual workshops to traditional books. Online platforms like Coursera, Udemy, and even free content on YouTube offer vast opportunities to gain new skills or deepen existing ones. By scheduling specific times each week for learning, individuals can create a consistent routine that naturally integrates education into daily life. Whether it's dedicating a few hours every weekend to study a new language or spending evenings reading industry-related articles, these practices help build a robust foundation for growth (Beckford, 2023).

In addition to structured learning formats, it's crucial to embrace change as a catalyst for personal development. Change often presents itself as an unfamiliar and challenging force; however, viewing it through a lens of opportunity can shift perceptions. Reflecting on past experiences and extracting lessons from them enables individuals to adapt more effectively to new situations. For instance, facing unexpected job responsibilities may initially seem daunting, yet it provides a chance to develop leadership skills and increase competency. By welcoming change with open arms, individuals position themselves to harness new possibilities and improve their adaptability (Wartoft, 2024).

Furthermore, creating a safe space for experimentation is vital in building resilience. Mistakes and setbacks should be viewed as integral components of the learning journey rather than indicators of failure. By reframing setbacks as valuable learning experiences, individuals cultivate patience and perseverance. This perspective allows them to explore new ideas without the fear of failure potentially stifling innovation. Whether attempting a novel project at work or pursuing a creative hobby, embracing trial and error fortifies one's ability to handle uncertainties and fosters confidence in navigating the unknown.

The integration of technology into daily learning routines offers another powerful tool for staying informed and relevant. Educational apps, podcasts, and e-learning platforms provide instant access to global knowledge pools, enabling learners to keep up with the latest industry trends. Using mobile apps such as Khan Academy or Duolingo during commutes transforms travel time into valuable learning opportunities.

Podcasts on topics of interest, played during workouts or chores, seamlessly integrate learning into everyday life. This tech-driven approach empowers individuals to maintain an ongoing dialogue with current developments, ensuring their skills remain sharp and applicable in changing environments.

Technology's role in facilitating continuous learning extends beyond just accessing information; it also encompasses engaging with interactive communities. Social media platforms and forums allow learners to connect with peers and experts worldwide, enriching the learning experience through shared insights and discussions. Networking with individuals who are already applying cutting-edge tools in practice can illuminate real-world applications and inspire fresh perspectives. Leveraging these connections fosters collaborative learning environments and enhances the overall effectiveness of acquiring new knowledge (Wartoft, 2024).

Establishing clear learning objectives further enhances the efficacy of this continuous growth mindset. Setting specific goals for skill acquisition helps focus efforts and track progress over time. These objectives serve as motivational benchmarks, encouraging a sense of accomplishment as milestones are reached. Additionally, breaking larger goals into smaller, manageable tasks makes the learning process less overwhelming and more approachable. Regularly revisiting and adjusting goals ensures they remain aligned with evolving personal and professional aspirations (Beckford, 2023).

Ultimately, nurturing a culture of curiosity and embracing uncertainty as a natural part of growth requires conscious effort and dedication. By creating an environment where learning is an integral part of everyday life, individuals cultivate the adaptability needed to navigate dynamic landscapes successfully. Encouraging an attitude of continuous improvement not only enhances intellectual acuity but also enriches emotional intelligence by fostering empathy and understanding.

Cultivate Resilience Through Continuous Self-Improvement

Enhancing resilience and overall well-being is crucial as we navigate life's many challenges. By adopting self-improvement practices, individuals can build a foundation of strength to adapt and thrive in both personal and professional spheres. One effective method for enhancing resilience is through regular self-reflection techniques, such as journaling. Journaling allows us to document our growth and assess our progress over time, fostering a deeper understanding of our experiences and learning. Research supports that expressive writing, including journaling, reduces stress, anxiety, and depression while improving emotional regulation and problem-solving skills (Journaling to Increase Self-Awareness, n.d.).

To start, consider maintaining a consistent journaling routine. You might begin by setting aside a few minutes each day or week to write down your thoughts, experiences, and reflections. Use this time to explore what you've learned, the obstacles you've overcome, and areas where you see potential for growth. Through journaling, you'll uncover patterns in your thoughts and behaviors, which can lead to improved decision-making and increased self-awareness. Over time, this practice builds mental clarity and fosters emotional resilience.

Another important aspect of enhancing resilience is developing a growth mindset. Stanford psychologist Carol Dweck introduced this concept as the belief that abilities and intelligence can be cultivated with dedication and hard work (Hopler, 2024). Embracing challenges as opportunities for development encourages us to view setbacks not as failures but as valuable learning experiences. Surrounding yourself with positive influences and supportive environments further nurtures this mindset. Engaging in communities or networks that share similar goals allows for the exchange of ideas, inspiration, and encouragement in overcoming obstacles.

Practicing gratitude is another powerful tool for strengthening resilience and emotional well-being. By regularly listing things you are thankful for, you can shift focus from negative stressors to the positive aspects of your life. This simple act of gratitude fosters emotional resilience and strengthens social connections. It cultivates an appreciation for everyday experiences and interactions, promoting a more optimistic outlook on life. Many people find that keeping a gratitude journal helps them stay mindful of the blessings and kindness they encounter daily.

Mindfulness and emotional regulation skills are also key elements in managing stress effectively. Techniques such as meditation, deep breathing exercises, or yoga can help individuals gain control over their responses to stressful situations. These practices encourage present-moment awareness and reduce impulsive reactions, leading to more thoughtful and composed actions. By incorporating mindfulness into daily routines, individuals can improve their capacity to handle pressure and maintain emotional balance. Additionally, seeking support when needed, whether through therapy or supportive friends and family, is vital in ensuring overall mental health and resilience.

Join Communities of Like-Minded Individuals for Support

In today's fast-paced world, it becomes increasingly vital to find ways to sustain personal growth and maintain motivation. One of the most impactful methods is through community support, which offers a rich ecosystem of resources, inspiration, and mutual encouragement. Community plays a crucial role, as highlighted by Prateek Gupta in "The Power of Community in Personal Growth: A Comprehensive Guide," where it is described as a pivotal element in shaping personal development (Gupta, 2024). By embedding oneself in the fabric of a supportive community, individuals can engage with others who share similar goals, set and pursue ambitious objectives together, and lay the groundwork for lifelong growth.

Connecting with like-minded individuals forms the backbone of utilizing community support effectively. Whether through local groups or online platforms, these connections allow individuals to engage in activities that resonate with their personal interests. Joining a local hobby club, an online forum, or a professional association can provide access to diverse perspectives and new ideas. These environments not only encourage shared learning experiences but also foster friendships based on mutual interests, creating bonds that serve as a constant source of motivation and inspiration.

Another effective strategy within community support involves establishing accountability partners to set and achieve mutual goals. Accountability partners act as motivators, reminding each other of commitments and celebrating successes together. This collaborative approach can be particularly beneficial when facing setbacks, as having someone to discuss challenges with can lead to fresh insights and innovative solutions. Sharing victories and hurdles fosters a deeper understanding and reinforces commitment to personal development, pushing individuals to persevere even in challenging times.

Engaging in workshops and events provides additional opportunities to network with like-minded individuals while leveraging community resources for skill enhancement. Attending seminars, conferences, or webinars opens doors to knowledge that might otherwise remain inaccessible. Such events are often breeding grounds for new relationships and provide practical skills applicable to one's personal or professional life. Participating in these activities can significantly enhance one's capabilities, ultimately contributing to sustained growth and development.

Mentorship programs also form an integral part of community support. They offer valuable insights and advice from those who have traversed similar paths before. Mentors can provide guidance on navigating career challenges, making informed decisions, and identifying opportunities for advancement. Moreover, by mentoring others, individuals reinforce their personal knowledge and contribute to the growth of their community. According to an article on overcoming barriers to successful mentoring, leaders can create environments that enhance mentor-mentee relationships by addressing common challenges such as workload management and cultural resistance (Usanmaz, 2023).

Overcoming fear of failure is another essential aspect of engaging with community support. Embracing failure as a natural part of the learning process allows individuals to take risks, explore new possibilities, and learn invaluable lessons. Creating a safe space for experimentation is crucial in fostering resilience. Encouraging self-compassion and patience during this journey ensures that individuals remain focused and committed to their personal development goals, even when faced with temporary setbacks.

Community support encourages the growth of a robust network, comprising mentors, peers, and colleagues, expanding one's access to invaluable resources and expertise. Such networks can facilitate diverse perspectives and innovative ideas, contributing to greater personal and professional success. For young adults entering adulthood or college students managing educational pressures, these networks offer critical support systems that help balance life's demands while enhancing mental health and well-being.

Stay Updated with New Research and Insights

In an ever-evolving world, staying updated with new knowledge and research is essential for personal growth. Lifelong learning is not just a concept but a necessity for young adults, college students, and young professionals who are navigating the complexities of adulthood, education, and careers. To thrive in these settings, it's important to actively engage in learning by remaining informed about the latest developments and trends in your areas of interest.

First and foremost, one effective strategy to stay informed is by following relevant journals and blogs. These platforms offer valuable insights into various fields, including mental health and personal development. By critically engaging with such content, you can broaden your understanding and remain abreast of current discussions. The sheer volume of articles available on these topics can be overwhelming, yet apps like Researcher help filter this information based on your interests, keeping your feed personalized and relevant (Team, 2022). Furthermore, reading reputed psychology journals or health blogs ensures that you're accessing credible information, which is crucial for making informed decisions about your personal development journey.

Another way to foster active engagement in learning is by experimenting with new techniques in your daily routines. Incorporating what you've learned from research or expert recommendations can be enlightening. For instance, trying out journaling as a method to boost mental well-being or integrating mindfulness practices into your routine could lead to surprising benefits (Journaling for Therapy and Mental Health: Benefits, Techniques, and 10 Prompts to Use | SonderMind, 2021). The key is to maintain curiosity and openness to emerging findings. This willingness to experiment not only reinforces learning but also builds resilience, as you learn to adapt and evolve through trial and error.

Furthermore, engaging with professionals through talks and webinars provides invaluable insights into the latest trends and innovations. These events offer a platform where experts share their knowledge, experiences, and future predictions, which can inspire and motivate attendees to apply newfound insights to their personal growth paths. Participating in webinars hosted by industry leaders or attending sessions led by researchers can greatly enhance your understanding of complex subjects. Moreover, these interactions allow for the exchange of ideas and networking, which is beneficial for career advancement and personal development alike.

In addition to external sources of learning, fostering discussions within your personal networks is equally significant. Sharing knowledge and exploring innovative ideas with peers encourages a culture of learning and development. Engaging in meaningful conversations not only helps solidify what you've learned but also exposes you to diverse perspectives. Cultivating such discussions within your circle can lead to collaborative problem-solving and creative thinking. It emphasizes the importance of community and the shared journey of lifelong learning. Discussing topics like mental health strategies or personal growth techniques with friends or colleagues can prove to be quite enriching, as it opens up avenues for mutual growth and support.

Leveraging technology plays a crucial role in enhancing learning to fit our modern lifestyles. Utilizing apps designed for educational purposes provides accessible content across various fields. Platforms like Google Scholar or academic social networks such as ResearchGate and Academia.edu facilitate seamless access to the latest research output, allowing you to follow the work of fellow researchers or professionals you admire. This networked approach not only keeps you informed but also connects you with educators and mentors digitally, offering guidance and mentorship opportunities.

Incorporating these practices into your life requires consistency and dedication. Regularly setting aside time to read, attend webinars, or engage with your network will ensure that you remain committed to personal development. Remember, lifelong learning is not a sprint but a marathon; the continuous acquisition of new knowledge and skills enriches your life and propels you towards your goals. Embracing these methods to stay updated places you on the right track for sustained growth and momentum in your personal and professional endeavors.

Summary and Reflections

As you move forward on your journey of personal development, remember that life constantly evolves, presenting us with new challenges and opportunities. Embracing lifelong learning and building resilience are key to navigating these changes successfully. By adopting a mindset that values continuous education and adaptability, you set the stage for ongoing growth and self-improvement. Whether through formal education, online resources, or simply exploring new interests and hobbies, there are countless ways to integrate learning into your daily routine. These practices not only enhance your skills but also build confidence, equipping you to handle the unexpected with grace.

Additionally, cultivating resilience is an essential companion to lifelong learning. As you encounter setbacks and obstacles, view them as stepping stones rather than roadblocks. Embrace change as a chance to develop your strengths and explore new possibilities. Surround yourself with supportive communities and engaging networks, where shared experiences can inspire and motivate you. Remember, it's important to be kind to yourself and allow room for trial and error along the way. This journey of self-discovery and growth is unique to each individual, so take it one step at a time, staying curious and open to what lies ahead.

17

Conclusion

As we reach the end of our journey together, let's take a moment to reflect on the mosaic of insights we've pieced together. This book has been more than just words on pages; it's a guidebook designed to accompany you through the labyrinth of early adulthood, offering tools and wisdom to help navigate its many twists and turns.

We began by delving into the foundation of mental health, laying the groundwork for everything that followed. Recognizing your emotional landscape is not just an academic exercise but a vital part of thriving amidst school pressures, work demands, and the intricacies of personal relationships. Understanding what emotions drive you—or hold you back—allows you to tackle daily challenges with resilience and grace. Imagine each strategy shared in these pages as a brick contributing to the strong fortifications of your life, shaping a space where happiness and wellness can flourish.

This is your life, after all, and fashioning it into a masterpiece requires dedication and practice. Achieving a balanced lifestyle isn't about temporary fixes or short-lived bursts of enthusiasm; it's about sustained, lifelong practice. Consider how a musician refines their melody through constant rehearsal, pushing beyond the pursuit of perfection and instead focusing on progress. Each small act of self-care, every positive interaction and mindful pause, contributes incrementally to a more harmonious existence. Embrace the steady rhythm of growth, knowing that consistency—imperfect as it may be—is your ally.

But this journey isn't one you need to walk alone. We've discussed how strengthening your inner world impacts your outer interactions. Every effort you make to build emotional resilience has ripples, touching those around you and deepening connections. Whether you're supporting a colleague through a tough project or sharing a quiet moment with a friend, these skills enhance empathy and understanding. Think of each interaction as a bridge, a conduit through which hearts connect and grow closer. When you integrate these practices into every facet of your life, you'll not only bolster your personal growth but also contribute to building a supportive community around you.

Life, undoubtedly, will continue to throw curveballs your way. Yet, embedded in these very challenges are opportunities waiting to unfold. This book encourages you to redefine setbacks, framing them as pivotal moments ripe for personal development. A difficult conversation at work isn't just a conflict to be dreaded; it's a chance to deepen your communication skills and forge stronger bonds. Approaching life's inevitable hurdles with empathy and clarity transforms potential stumbling blocks into stepping stones. Remember, the rain that prompts a flower to blossom is the same downpour that might initially appear as a storm—it's all about perspective.

When you embrace this mindset, you become a creator of your own destiny. Think about how powerful that truly is. With every page you've turned, you've been crafting a toolkit filled with strategies to enrich your mind and nourish your soul. You're ready to sculpt the life you envision, armed with insights tailored for young adults, college students, and budding professionals alike. No matter the path you choose, these lessons remain evergreen, encouraging you to keep evolving, learning, and growing.

Imagine meeting future challenges with confidence, rooted in the knowledge that you have the resources to thrive. Picture yourself engaging with classmates, colleagues, family, and friends from a place of strength and understanding. Think about transforming stresses and strains into creative forces that propel you forward. By turning these pages, you've already taken a significant step toward realizing this vision.

The beauty of life is that it's a continuous journey with no definitive endpoint. You'll carry these learnings with you, adapting and reshaping them as you evolve. There will be days when things fall effortlessly into place, and others when they feel like uphill battles. In both instances, remind yourself of the importance of persistence and patience. You're charting a course uniquely your own, grounded in the principles of well-being and personal growth that we've explored together.

As you close this chapter, open wide the possibilities ahead. Let the insights from this book serve as your compass, guiding you through new experiences and unfamiliar territories. You're equipped not merely to survive, but to thrive—to transform aspirations into realities and dreams into achievements. The narrative you've begun here will continue to unfold, rich with promise and potential.

Above all, remember that you're not alone. Countless peers are walking similar paths, and though the trails diverge and intersect, there's comfort in shared experiences. Lean into the connections you've fostered along the way and draw inspiration from the stories of others. Life's greatest adventures arise from moments of vulnerability and courage, intertwined with the spirit of community and cooperation.

So, go forth with an open mind and a brave heart. Embrace the unknown with curiosity and the known with gratitude. May these reflections serve as a reminder of the strength within you, lying patiently beneath the surface, ready to rise to the occasion. Whatever you embark upon next, know that you have the capacity to shape it beautifully and profoundly. Thank you for allowing this book to accompany you; the next chapter of your story awaits, full of endless possibilities.